Somebody BIGGER!

A Handbook of God Wows

Nita Weis, Ph.D.

Dedication

Somebody Bigger is dedicated to all those who made precious time withdrawals from their busy work and family schedules in order to read the book prior to publication. I'm enormously grateful for their proof suggestions…and humbled by their encouraging, kind review comments.

I'd also like to dedicate *Somebody Bigger* to the most important people in my *earthly* life…my children, Kevin, Kendall, Leesa, and Lori. Their spiritual walk with the Lord makes me thankful every day. Their humor continues to make me smile. When they tell me I'm a role model, it makes me feel better about myself and definitely is a *memory keeper!* I know they're always in my front-row cheering section, delighted I'm doing something with purpose…that I also love.

Most important of all, *Somebody Bigger: A Handbook of God Wows* is dedicated to God, to be used for His purpose alone. My prayer is that the *God Wows* will help Christians make a more significant impact as they share their stories of faith with non-believers.

Nita Weis, 2014

Table of Contents

Introduction

"Who is like the Lord our God, who dwells on high?"
Psalm 113:5

Somebody Bigger (SB) is simply a little handbook of *God Wows*—proof of *Intelligent Design* evidenced by God's creation for which there can be only one response, *Wow! SB* will present only <u>some</u> of *God's Wows,* because *all the volumes in the world could not contain ALL of them!* (John 21:25)

I think you'd agree with me that gathering information is tedious and time consuming for everyone. Being legally blind until age fifteen made this task a particularly-unique problem for me, forcing me to glean all the good stuff from printed sources in short spurts of *"seeing"* time. This early appreciation for concise presentation of material continued into my doctoral studies, as I received honors for a paper on *"Concise Communication, Construct for Contemporary Culture."* So, I promise to be *concise* as I select, categorize, condense, and simplify 1000's of *God-Wow factoids*...using the six days of creation as a guide.

God graciously answered my prayers and granted my surgeons the skills that restored my eyesight to 20/20 vision. Along with it, I believe He gave me a heightened appreciation and visual sensitivity to see God in nature. I never see a *so-so* sunset or a *ho-hum* bouquet of Hyacinths. I am forever in awe at the beauty and aroma of cascading Lilacs weaving their way through a trellis, and the lavender-laced umbrellas of Jacaranda trees still take my breath away. I pray that my wonder and appreciation of God's infinite color pallet will never be satiated.

I make no personal claim for any *new discoveries* in SB. Credit for the *God-Wow* information presented is *edited* from the research of many specialists in their fields—scientists, astronomers, medical professionals, mathematicians, and Bible scholars. Excerpts from various *creation, astronomy, nature,* and *oceanography* websites supplied the interesting quick facts. My primary role was that of fact-gathering and organizing the *God Wows* into a *handbook* that believers could use in sharing their faith with others.

Some of the *God Wows screamed* for pictorial representation, so I am enormously grateful to the various websites that offered the *free-stock photos* used. Credit for the resources used during my research for SB is given within the text or at the end of the book.

Chapter one begins with my own satirical spoof on evolution, but be assured that SB is much more than a brief review of *Creation vs. Evolution.* Although this issue has been written about, debated, and discussed by scholars from both sides, I must admit that I strongly disagree with some of my Christian friends who think it's irrelevant whether or not God used *evolution* to create man. If we accept the *theoretical* premise that man *evolved* from apes, we do away with *original sin*…and the subsequent need for our Savior, Jesus Christ.

My goal in writing SB is to provide believers with a *user-friendly, Intelligent-Designer reference tool* to use in their witness to the *"nones."* This is a term I use for *the questioning and the denying* crowds—those who think they're smarter than God...perhaps also having taken a proverbial bite out of Eve's forbidden fruit!

Even though believers are not responsible for those who choose *not* to believe in our Creator, the Bible does tell us to be ready with answers and reasons for our beliefs. My prayer is that this *little handbook of God Wows* helps you make a spiritually-significant impact as you interact with the *questioning and denying crowd* in the workplace, schools and universities, social gatherings...and sadly even in some churches! And as you read through SB, may I suggest that you keep a highlighter handy to make it easier to find some of your favorite *God Wows to share.*

> *"Always be prepared to give an answer to everyone who asks you to give the reason for the hope that you have, but do it with gentleness and respect."* 1 Peter 3:15

Nita Weis

Chapter One

Just By Chance...*They* Say

The fool says in his heart, "There is no God."
Psalm 14:1

I'd had several news articles published before, authored a few books and educational materials, so I felt fairly confident about submitting my article to a rather large newspaper as a guest columnist. It also was to be my writing *debut* using satire to make a point.

Much to my disappointment, the editor opted *not* to publish it, and I was curious about his reason for rejecting the article. Was it the writing style; was it my obvious *creationist* stance; or was it purely a pre-emptive decision to avert backlash from those of the newspaper-subscriber base that wave the banner for *evolution*? At the time, my guess was the latter. But in hindsight, I think that the Lord may have had a different purpose and reader audience in mind all along—as the springboard to *Somebody Bigger*. So, let's poke some gigantic holes in the theory of evolution while you grade me on my use of satire!

Just By Chance...They Say!

Let me see if I understand this. Evolutionists say that in the beginning, a *Big Bang* occurred, setting off this mechanical dance of atoms, forming a big vat of pre-biotic soup, from which a tadpole wiggled, and *voila*, amoebas became astronauts, cantaloupes became kittens, and monkeys became men…a few million or so years later…*just by chance, they say!*

Let's talk "small" for a minute. We're told by those who are good at really detail stuff and counting *really, really* small things, that the human body consists of over thirty trillion single cells, each cell so tiny that a million of them occupy a space about the size of the period at the end of this sentence. Yet every human being originates from just *ONE* cell, in union with *ONE* sperm. Then this squiggly little blueprint for life tells the body how to reproduce itself and even to some degree, heal itself. Using twenty-first century technology, scientists have now studied the complexity and functionality of microscopic *single cells* under 50,000 times magnification. What they discovered is a *micro-miniaturized factory*, by far more complicated than any machinery ever *imagined* or built by man. And I'm to believe this is all…*just by chance, you say?*

Let's talk about memory…before I forget. We're learning that man's brain—the entire body's *command center*—is the most complex computer ever studied. Still we know very little about this phenomenal organ and its infinite capabilities. Man's brain enables him to dream, plan ahead, create, respond, imagine, problem solve, explore the universe, and produce a series of emotions from compassion and love, to sorrow, fear, hate, and self-defense.

Scientists calculate that the brain's grey matter contains over 100 billion cells called neurons. Each neuron then connects to between 1000 and 10,000 synapses. It's along these miniature, yet massive connections that our brains have recorded and stored—ready for the most efficient retrieval—*every* stimulus our sensory organs have *ever* perceived throughout our lives. (I must confess that my own retrieval system occasionally needs some *tweaking*.) What the brain does next are some tasks that boggle the mind. It monitors each sensory impulse, makes a split, millisecond analysis, then sends out information to the appropriate command post for an instantaneous response. No *error messages*, no wait time for *booting up...*just *instant access to limitless RAM. Wow! All this...just by chance, they say!*

Let's think upside-down. Take the Bat, voted most likely *NOT* to become the favorite collectible by even the quirkiest of kids. However, it is one of the most interesting to study. As the Bat sleeps, hanging *upside down*, its brain cells likely get a good blood bath from gravity's pull. The Bat is now refreshed and ready for his upcoming flight task—finding its way in total darkness—*flying blind*, so to speak. Using an elaborate system of sound vibrations, the Bat navigates by sending out high-pitched, ultrasonic signals from its vocal organs that bounce off anything in its path. Then, at lightning speed, the Bat's brain analyzes these signals and makes the necessary *flight-and-food-catching responses* to these signals that prevent him from flying into walls...thereby *keeping him in the Bat race... just by chance!*

Let's look at some missing-link mishaps. Around 1890, on the island of Java in Indonesia, Dr. Eugene Dubois announced to the world that he'd found the 500,000 year-old missing link—*brace yourself for this*—after unearthing *just the top of the skull, a piece of the thigh bone,* and *THREE TEETH.* Now, I admit that I'm not a paleontologist; I had to apply Spell Check to make sure I hadn't misspelled it! My doctorate is in Human Behavior, but I'd still like to offer you my perfunctory opinion of Dubois's *discovery.* Either he was under peer pressure to publish, or he was drinking way too much coffee when he found *Java Man. No pun intended!* Incidentally, Dr. Dubois eventually confessed that his *Pithecanthropus erectus* was just a *very-elderly monkey! News Flash:* I predict with reasonable certainty that an objective re-examination of *MOST* of the *so-called facts* in evolution will continue to expose even more of *these banana-loving, senior swingers!*

In 1917, Harold Cook, a rancher and geologist in Nebraska, discovered the *Nebraska Man*...correction, *found ONE TOOTH!* You heard right...*ONE TOOTH!* Cook went on to suggest incredulously that this *Nebraska dude* was 1,000,000 years old! Stretching incredulity to the max, he then extrapolated an entire race of men and women...from *ONE TOOTH!* (I hate to admit it, but when compared to Cook's discovery, Dubois's work begins to look like a scientific breakthrough—his find included *THREE TEETH!*) Seriously, does this sound like there's a lot more missing here than *the missing link* between ape and man? *You think?* Here's what I think: I think that Cook *missed* his *real* calling—a promising career as a writer of science fiction!

Bear with me for one last example of scientific skullduggery...often referred to as one of the most famous frauds in the history of science. This one is the *infamous Eoanthropus Dawsonii,* more commonly known as the *Piltdown Man.* The long-story-shortened goes like this. Charles Dawson, a respected lawyer, spent the better part of six years digging around in Sussex England's Piltdown Gravel Pit. (You still may be able to find this pit using your GPS grid references.) Around 1912, after sustaining very dirty hands and fingernails, Charles found a *piece of jaw, TWO MOLAR TEETH, and a piece of a skull.* These fragments were tagged *"science"* with a big black marker, and for nearly a half-century, hundreds of thousands of school children have been reading textbooks filled with this spurious science about *Ole Pilt'.* It wasn't until 1953, that we learned that *Ole Pilt'* was just a hoax. *No Kidding! Ole Pilt'* was just a fifty-year-old ape with its teeth filed down and artificially colored! I guess Charlie wasn't about to leave this fraud to...*just chance.*

As an educator for over forty years, I find it's especially egregious that the minds of America's most precious and vulnerable resources are being polluted with unproven if not outright fraudulent information. Educators have the opportunity, responsibility and privilege to provide students with the most accurate information available, teaching them how to observe, research, question, and ultimately make their own responsible decisions. I agree with Swedish embryologist, Sorren Luthrip, who said, "I believe that one day the Darwinian myth will be ranked the greatest deceit in the history of science."

These pseudo-scientific *myths about evolution* could have been exposed long ago if it weren't for the *silence* of the estimated seventy-nine percent of Americans who identify themselves religiously as Christians or Jews. Our confidence that we hold the truth about *Creation* shames us as believers and Biblical scholars for not being more *collectively vocal*. This rather impressive majority accepts the *Genesis version of Creation in the Bible...*

> *"In the beginning, God created the heavens and the earth."* Genesis 1:1
>
> *"Thus the heavens and the earth were completed in all their vast array. By the seventh day, God had finished the work he had been doing; so on the seventh day he rested from all his work."* Genesis 2:1-2

From even a cursory examination of the sheer magnitude of this incredible universe and the countless and wondrous creations in it, where else could logic lead except to an awesome Creator? Or as physicist and mathematician Isaac Newton put it, "This most beautiful system of sun, planets and comets could only proceed from the council and dominion of an intelligent and powerful being."

I believe man was created by God...*in His own image!* I believe this not only *'because the Bible tells me so,'* and not only because the likes of Cook, Dawson, and Dubois failed the authenticity test; but because "evolution is not observable, repeatable, or refutable, and thus does not qualify as either a scientific fact or theory." (H. Lipson, Physicist, 1980) I'm a believer, a child of the King, and the beneficiary of God's love. The blood running though my veins is *Royal* blood, not the blood of monkeys! I guess it comes down to who's your Daddy, God or monkeys? It's your call.

Let's end with some simple logic. *"If"* everyone and everything in this universe is the result of a *BIG BANG*, it follows that there had to be a *BANG-OR*. When you look at a watch, you assume there was a watchmaker. As Sir John Templeton queried, "Would it not be strange if a universe without purpose accidentally created humans who are so obsessed with purpose?" It's not *just by chance,* so don't believe everything *"they say!"*

Chapter Two

God Did *What*...in *Six* Days?

"And God saw everything that He had made, and behold, it was very good. And the evening and the morning were the sixth day. Thus the heavens, and the earth were finished, and all the host of them."
Genesis 1:31; 2:1

The short answer is that God created this incredible, indescribable, mind-numbingly awesome universe and everything in it. *And,* yes, He did it in *just six days!*

Try wrapping your mind around the *immeasurable intelligence and power* that first *imagined,* then *spoke* the billions of stars into existence. *And*...astronomers continue to discover new galaxies as bigger and more powerful telescopes are developed. *And*...don't stop there. Think about the wisdom it took to design the complex laws that govern *ALL* of creation... from the smallest sub-atomic particle to the ever-expanding galaxies of outer space.

The next time you're at the mall, a sports event, or in a restaurant, take a look at the people around you to sample God's *infinite creativity* in original design. No two people are alike, not even identical twins. Each person has unique eye prints, voice prints, finger prints, and tongue prints...*yes even identical twins!* Imagine the Creator genius who with only a few basic *puzzle parts* to work with—two eyes, two ears, hair and skin color, facial shape, and bone structure—has and continues to execute <u>*billions of originals!!!*</u> God always thinks *outside* the box.

You may not live in an area that experiences a lot of extreme weather conditions. If not, watch the weather channel or the evening news during reports of severe weather when it's occurring somewhere else. You will observe God's *power* in nature…in the winds, hurricanes, storms, thunder and lightning, Tsunamis, and volcano eruptions.

> *"For since the creation of the world God's invisible qualities—his eternal power and divine nature—have been clearly seen, being understood from what has been made, so that men are without excuse."* Romans 1:20

You may be surprised to learn that Satan himself was the first to question God's authority and power when he spoke to Eve in the Garden of Eden. (Genesis 3:1-4) Today, we hear similar, just more contemporary arguments from atheists, humanists, *some* scientists, and modern-day progressives. Some of these groups smugly wear the banner of *"political correctness."* Others protest that this *six-day creation feat* is incredulous. However, a more honest *translation* of all their *protestations* exposes what's *really* behind their zeal. A world created by God—*in no matter how many days or millennia*—collides with their preconceived agenda of *disbelief in God, period!* Acknowledging a belief in God requires attitudes and behaviors that these groups are unwilling to accept—admission of personal sin, faith in God, humility, and kindness toward others.

Before we continue, let me say that I would never expect *anyone,* including myself, to accept God as the Creator without *undeniable proof.* In the chapters that follow, SB will provide some significant proof that *God IS God, He's uncontainably big, and infinitely smart...*and we're not! The Bible says that, *"...God winked at the ignorance of man...."* (Acts 17:30-31) While I'm not totally clear about what God's *wink* meant, I'm reasonably confident it's similar to a colloquialism my Mom used after I'd said something stupid, "My dear, what do you know? You're still wet behind the ears."

The cumulative *wisdom* of all mankind is still *finite* and earns only a *God wink* when compared to God's *infinite galaxies of knowledge!* That's why God is *worthy* of our worship. It's completely ludicrous for the creations from *"clay"* to question the infallible and incomprehensible intelligence, immeasurable power, and unfathomable ability of the *Creator-sculptor.* Those who dare to do this will be judged laughable *fools!* (Psalm 14:1)

Let's consider for a moment that you had signed up for a class entitled, *How the World Began.* How excited would you be to learn that the *Creator* himself would be teaching the course? It's obvious that the Creator of something is the best one to describe how He did it, right? Well, it just so happens that we have the next best thing—the *Creator's* own *"lecture-note revelations,"* thanks to the first few chapters in the book of Genesis, the first book of the Old Testament in the Bible. Many other books in the Old Testament also document the various creation events. *FYI...*it's also no coincidence that the word, *Genesis,* means *origins, source, or beginnings.*

By no stretch of the imagination am I *gullible* when it comes to accepting the *ridiculous, the deniable, or the unbelievable.* I'm happy to say that I find myself in the company of some 2.5 billion believing contemporaries worldwide, along with the hundreds of millions of Christians from past generations. One can find all the evidence needed to validate the limitless power, creativity, and majesty of an amazing God by doing any one of the *most common activities*—taking a walk barefoot on a sandy beach in the early evening; listening to the hypnotizing sounds of the ocean and its rhythmic waves; watching a breathtakingly beautiful sunset painted quickly on the *horizon canvas* in masterfully-mixed and ever-changing hues of red, yellow, burgundy, and purple; or gazing in amazement at the *countless galaxy* of twinkling stars in the velvet black sky...*the grand finale!*

We do need to clear up a few issues to answer the agnostics concerning the word, *day,* as it's used by God during the *Creation process* in the book of Genesis. We know that God is *Omniscient—all knowing* of things past and future, and that He didn't set Himself up to be blindsided by the backlash from the non-believing community. God didn't *wish in hindsight* that He'd made Himself clearer about *the literal six-days of creation.* Rather, it was in His *foreknowledge* that He made it *crystal* clear what He <u>meant</u> when He used the word, *day*—either a *literal 24-hour day,* or whether He meant *ages of time.*

For 1000s of years, the literal six-day creation was believed and taught by the Jews. Then the teachings of *progressive creationism* began to extend their insidious tentacles into the religious community under the guise of *reconciling* the conflict between evolution and creationism. Don't forget the devastating results of the world's *first compromise with truth* presented by Satan to Eve in the Garden of Eden—*sin passed to all men!* (Romans 5:12) Why should believers who hold the *true* account of Creation from the Bible even consider *tweaking* the words of Almighty God in an eternally-and-spiritually-disasterous attempt to align ourselves with unbelievers?

The word, *"day,"* in the Hebrew language is *"yom."* As a point of fact, *"yom"* <u>can</u> mean a literal twenty-four hour day. But it can *also* mean a set time period…

- Gen. 2:4   *the day*

- Lev. 14:2   *day that*

- Ps. 20:1   *day of trouble*

- Job 20:28   *day of his wrath*

- 2 Cor. 6:2   *day of salvation*

- Phil. 1:6   *day of Jesus Christ*

- Isa. 2:12   *day of Yahweh*

- 1 Cor. 5:5 *day of the Lord*

- Zeph. 1:10 *day of the Lord is at hand*

- Dan. 7:9-13 (the Lord is referred to as the) *Ancient of Days*

- 2 Pet. 3:8 *With the Lord, one day is as a 1000 years...*

- Ex. 20:11 *"For in six days the Lord made the heavens and the earth, the sea, and all that is in them, and rested the seventh day. Therefore the Lord blessed the Sabbath day and hallowed it."*

So, it's evident in the scripture examples given that the word *day* did have many meanings. *BUT,* whenever the word, *day,* is mentioned with a numeral next to it, it means the number mentioned...as is the case during the creation process in Genesis! Also, remember that Jews measured a day as *from sunset to sunset*.

Most believers think it's safer to simply take God at His word rather than try to interpret what He *really* meant. For example, in Genesis 5:5, we read that *"Adam lived 930 years, and then he died."* Think about this for a moment. If one day in the Genesis account represented a thousand years—or even a million as evolutionists believe—then how could we explain Adam's age? Adam lived 930 years, so if each year had approximately 360 days, that equals 360 million years. Multiply that total by 930 years old when he died, and Adam was then older than *ANY* estimated age of the earth or the universe!

Here are a few simple analogies that I've collected over the years that you might find useful with the *"nones"*—those agnostics, atheists, modern-day progressives, and evolutionists who think the world came about *without* a Creator…and that it was impossible that the world could have been created in less than billions of years.

- *So, you're saying, "Nothing times nobody equals everything…right?"*

- *Creation without a Creator—"The Big Bang Theory"—is like believing you could load the parts of a Cadillac into the cargo bay of a 747, dump them out at 30,000 feet, and expect them to be fully assembled upon impact.*

- *Scientists in a lab trying to prove God exists is like tearing apart a piano looking for a concerto.*

- *Believing there is no Creator is like expecting one to believe that an explosion of a printing press resulted in an unabridged dictionary.*

- *Creation without a Creator is the equivalent of believing that the Ceiling of the Sistine Chapel was the result of paint-by-number.*

- *Or as Shakespeare said, "Nothing comes of nothing!"*

Chapter Three

God's *First Day* at Work!

"He spoke and the world began."
Psalm 33:9

*"By faith we understand that the worlds were framed
by the word of God, so that the things which are seen
were not made of things which are visible"*
Hebrews 11:3

Do you remember your first day at work? Were you a bundle of nerves …unsure of your ability to perform all the tasks? On the other hand, you might have been filled with a rush of exhilaration and confidence, eager to prove to your parents and friends that you were ready to earn your *own* way in the adult world.

When you press your memory's *back-arrow* key to the first job for which you received a real paycheck, I hope your memory is a happier one than mine. Right after high-school graduation, my first summer job as the cashier at a drugstore lasted a whole half day! That roll of paper that prints out the cash-register receipts ran out after the first few transactions, and I was too embarrassed to ask someone to show me how to replace it. So, I *unprofessionally* abandoned my post at the register and walked off the job without a word of explanation to anyone. Trust me, this job experience never appeared on my resume. Now, let's take a look at what Genesis records about God's first day at work...

> *"And God said, let there be light, and there was light. God saw that the light was good, and He separated the light from the darkness. God called the light day, and the darkness He called night. And there was evening and there was morning—the first day."* Genesis 1:3-5

From our previous discussion of the word, *day,* used in creation events, notice how God makes it doubly clear that He created light that separated light from darkness *in a day,* by stressing *"...there was evening and there was morning—the first day."*

Physicists reported in 2013 that *"dark matter"* makes up approximately 23 percent of the universe. *Ordinary matter*—that's you and me—makes up only 4 percent of the universe. Physicists theorize that the remaining 73 percent consists of mysterious *"dark energy."* Sounds to me like the scientists are *still in the dark* about a big majority of what's out there in the universe!

So, *does darkness exist; can it be measured, and how does it affect us?* The answer to the first question is *yes, darkness exists*, but darkness is simply *the absence of light*. So, darkness *cannot be measured;* we can only measure light. Consider what Jesus said about light and darkness, *"I am the light of the world. Whoever follows me will not walk in darkness, but will have the light of life."* John 8:12

Let's look for a moment at what made God's *first day of work* so special and how light and darkness affect us. Did you ever stop to think about what it would be like to be *really in the dark?* I'm talking pitch-black darkness you can *feel or cut with a knife!* I recall reading a magazine article about the early days of space exploration. The astronauts in training were placed in floating devices in water in a completely-dark, totally-soundproof chamber. After a few hours in this light-deprived environment, the astronauts were unable to report with any degree of accuracy how long they'd been in the room.

Psychiatrists also have conducted many studies on the effects on the human psyche from total-light deprivation. One experiment required eight volunteers to remain in total darkness for a forty-eight hour period. One member—a comedian named Bloom—reported a particularly interesting experience forty-eight hours after his release. A comparison of his before-and-after psychological tests results showed clear impairment of his ability to process information, a reduction in memory, and also an increase in suggestibility. But for Bloom, there was another and unexpected outcome. He said that upon arriving at the bunker *before* the experiment, he'd assessed the bunker surroundings as being rather bleak. The exterior was all overgrown, and basically the bunker was an eyesore. But when he left after forty-eight hours, he saw things much differently. Here's the shortened version he gave…

"The grass was now greener, the sky was bluer, and I now saw hundreds of yellow buttercups. Things now appeared staggeringly beautiful; even washing my hands under the tap was amazing. I made a vow that I would never fail to notice and appreciate my surroundings again. I'm glad I did it, but no sum of money would convince me to go through forty-eight hours on my own again. It was the greatest endurance test of my life."

Just as astronauts and members of psychiatric studies report impairment of mental ability from light deprivation, Christians need to be reminded that our friends, neighbors, relatives, and co-workers remain in *"eternal darkness"* without belief and trust in the One who gives *"eternal light"* to those who ask.

"This is the message we have heard from him and proclaim to you, that God is light, and in him is no darkness at all. If we say we have fellowship with him while we walk in darkness, we lie and do not practice the truth. But if we walk in the light, as he is in the light, we have fellowship with one another, and the blood of Jesus his Son cleanses us from all sin." 1 John 1:5-7

Think for a moment what you would be missing if you lived in darkness...even for a short period of time. For example, if you lived in Alaska, you would experience the longest day of the year in the United States, and there's no sunset for eighty-two days in summer. Alaska also has the longest night with no sunrise for sixty-seven days in winter.

I think we all agree that we're okay with *darkness* when it's time to go to sleep, but no one would choose darkness over light...*all the time.* It's impossible to imagine anything more glorious than waking in the morning to the *light* of God's awesome universe to observe...

- Warm sunrises that announce the morning...

- Snow-capped mountain peaks...

- Lush green rain forests...

- Crashing waves and crimson sunsets...

- Rainbow ribbons after rainstorms...

- Birds arrayed in brilliant-multicolored feather masterpieces...

- Fields of wild Blue Bonnets and acres of Poppies...

- The delicate design of an Orchid...

- Fairy-like flights of multicolored Monarch Butterflies

- Trees displaying their autumn-leaf collection...

- The majestic rock formations of Wyoming, Montana, & Utah

- The golden-curl-wrapped chubby cheeks of a smiling baby...

- The entertaining antics of dogs and kittens.....

- Billowing, ever-changing cloud formations floating across azure skies...

- Herds of buffalo and wild horses kicking up clouds of dust and turf...

- The Betsy Bug crawling across a child's outstretched palm...

We can see that God's first day at work had enormous implications for our planet and everything in it that He created. Without light, His next creations would not have been able to survive—the sun by its heat and light performing a thousand miracles a day in the plant kingdom through photosynthesis. And without the *Light of the world,* we would be in eternal darkness. God had a *six-day plan* for creating the universe, and the sequence of each day's work was specific and purposeful.

Chapter Four

Day Two: Water Engineer Extraordinaire!

"Who has wrapped up the waters in a cloak?"
Proverbs 30:4b

Let's say you had a degree in Civil and Environmental Engineering and you saw the following job posting in the *Global Herald News,* would you have the confidence to apply?

Water-Resource Engineer for Planet Earth

> *Job Description*: Design, build, implement a sustainable infrastructure for Planet Earth. Applicant must have advanced Civil Engineering Degree and application must demonstrate knowledge that includes detailed specifications and calculations for a comprehensive, full-scale, self-supporting, and sustainable water system of all needs for the *as-yet-to-be-defined life* of Planet Earth. This self-sustaining water system must include and fully support the food and water-supply needs of *all* mankind for drinking, bathing, cleaning, cooking; the needs of all vegetation; the needs of all animal and marine life; the needs of all domestic, industrial, manufacturing, commercial cleaning, and disaster clean-up.

God, who is the *Water Engineer Extraordinaire*, fulfilled the job description perfectly...*in one day!* He began with His simple but perfect components—two atoms of hydrogen and one of oxygen. *All water everywhere is the same*, reminding us that all chemical reactions require the exact computations of an intelligent being.

Then, God said, "Let there be a space between the waters, to separate the waters of the heavens from the waters of the earth. And that is what happened. God made this space to separate the waters of the earth from the waters of the heavens. God called the space, 'sky.' And evening passed and morning came, marking the second day." Genesis 1:6-8

Incidentally, the *space* between the heavens and earth mentioned in this scripture passage refers to a separation of the waters here on earth from the mists in the atmosphere of the skies. The mention of this *space* for separation of waters is significant, as you'll read in some of the water-fact statistics that follow.

Here's a simple question to ask your unbelieving friends at the water cooler. *Can you explain how it came about that the water of every ocean, sea, lake, and pond corresponds with the exact sphericity of the earth?* It would make no difference whether you gave them a week or a millennium to come up with their answer. It's simply impossible for our *finite* minds to even imagine the intricacy and intelligence of the *Divine Mind* that could envision all the necessary calculations of planet earth's water system. Here's just one remarkable example. Scientists tell us that water contracts as the temperature falls. But within four degrees of the freezing point, water expands and ice becomes lighter than water…and floats! This is significant, because this fact prevents all bodies of water from becoming solid bodies of ice. Who but the *Executive Director of the Universe* could have known how to design this?

It's been estimated that every second about 16,000,000 tons of rain and snow fall to the earth, and God calculates the paths of each snowflake and raindrop instantly and unerringly. Just *reading* about the following, interesting water facts would stagger the minds of even the most renowned civil, environmental, or geospatial engineers. But God's mind of amazing power, intelligence, and foreknowledge enabled Him to complete His water plan on His *second* day at work...*no need for a calculator!*

I want to acknowledge and thank Reader's Digest, World Water Council, NY Times, and Florida Environmental Association *for the selected water facts that follow.* Keep in mind that the following lists *just a few* of the water-need facts God had to *know* and factor into His *perfect* creation and design of planet earth.

- Water covers 70.9% of the earth's surface.

- 1.7% of the world's water is frozen and unusable.

- Only 3% of the earth's water is fresh water...*potable or drinkable.*

- 97% of the water on earth is salt water.

- The water found at the earth's surface in lakes, rivers, streams, ponds, and swamps makes up only 0.3% of the world's fresh water.

- 68.7% of the fresh water on earth is trapped in glaciers.

- 30% of fresh water is in the ground.

- There is more fresh water in the atmosphere than in all of the rivers on the planet combined.

- If all the water vapor in the earth's atmosphere fell at once and was distributed evenly, it would only cover the earth with about an inch of water.

- Approximately 400 billion gallons of water are used in the United States per day.

- Nearly one-half of the water used by Americans is used for thermoelectric power generation.

- In one year, the average American residence uses over 100,000 gallons of water indoors and outside.

- It takes seven and a half years for the average American residence to use the same amount of water that flows over the Niagara Falls in one second—750,000 gallons.

- It takes more water to manufacture a new car, 39,090 gallons, than to fill an above ground swimming pool.

- It takes more than ten gallons of water to produce one slice of bread.

- Over 713 gallons of water go into the production of one cotton T-shirt.

- 1000 gallons of water are required to produce one gallon of milk.

- Roughly 634 gallons of water go into the production of one hamburger.

- Water is the only substance found on earth naturally in three forms—solid, liquid, and gas.

- Water makes up between 55-78% of a human's body weight.

- An estimated 2.2 million plant and animal species find space to live in oceans.

- Another 6.5 million plant and animal species that live on land also need water.

- Scientists continue to search for the estimated 86% of existing species on land and 91% of species in the ocean that still await description.

On average, sixty-five percent of the human body is made up of water. Water is essential to blood that carries oxygen and nutrients to cells and for flushing wastes out of our bodies. Water cushions our joints and soft tissues. Without water as a routine part of our intake, we would be unable to digest or absorb food. We can survive three minutes without air, three days without water, and three weeks without food. But despite this *survival rule of three,* we've probably all read about people rescued from rubble after an earthquake, flood, or some other catastrophe who survived up to eight to ten days without water. So whether it's three days or eight-to-ten days, *the human body cannot survive without water.* I'm sure it was no accident that Jesus designed the importance of water into man's survival...and many times He likened it to eternal life.

But whoever drinks of the water that I shall give him will never thirst. But the water that I shall give him will become in him a fountain of water springing up into everlasting life." John 4:14

Chapter Five

Day Three: Earth, God's Concerto

"My own hand laid the foundations of the earth, and my right hand spread out the heavens; when I summon them, they all stand up together."
Isaiah 48:13

Nothing on the earth is ever at rest. Our Milky Way Galaxy is rotating at 225 km per second, hurling through the cosmos at an estimated 305 km per second. Adding these figures together, and we're racing through space at some 330 miles per second. In one minute, we've traveled almost 12,000 miles!

Scientists tell us that the earth turns noiselessly every 24 hours, at the rate of 1000 miles an hour, without the loss of even a second in 1000 years. The earth travels around the sun at the rate of 18.5 miles per second—75 times faster than a cannon ball load of 6,600,000,000,000,000,000,000 tons. The earth always arrives at a given point in its orbit at the exact time every year! The orbit of the earth is so vast that it varies from a straight line only 4 inches in 666 miles—the distance from Philadelphia to Chicago. It's either a madman or a fool who thinks this massive, spinning home to billions of plants, animals, humankind (and, let's not forget the 70 percent water) could maintain its orbit in space *without God's infinite power, planning, and intelligence!*

In Genesis 1:9-13, we find the full account of God's *third day* of creation—the earth, sea, grass, herbs that yield seeds, and fruit trees. Let's begin by examining some quick facts about this incredible globe of *spinning* real estate that God designed as a temporary dwelling place for His most precious creation, man.

Planet earth is not out there in space *spinning* alone! Astronomers tell us that our Milky Way measures up to 120,000 light years across, and they estimate that it contains up to 400 billion stars! They also report that our Milky Way teams with billions—*that's with a B*—of planets that are about the size of the earth. These billions of planets orbit stars just like our sun. And that's just a tip of the universe. Astronomers also say there are probably more than 170 billion galaxies in the "observable" universe that stretch out into a space 13.8 billion light years away in all directions. So, if you're of the mathematical persuasion, that computes to a *septillion stars!*

In a study published in the proceedings of the National Academy of Science (November 4, 2013), scientists reported finding 833 new-candidate planets with NASA's (now-crippled) Kepler space telescope. Discovery of these new planets brings the total to 3,538, although most could not support life. The Kepler space telescope has identified 10 planets about the size of earth, circling sun-like stars. Their mathematical calculations say that in our Milky Way galaxy alone, there are 8.8 billion planets. For perspective, *that's more earth-like planets than there are people on earth!* The Hubble Space Telescope sends back infrared images of faint galaxies that are perhaps 12 billion light years away—*that's 12 billion x 6 trillion miles away!* Astronomers venture a feeble estimate that *the number of stars in the universe equals the number of grains of sand on all the beaches of the world!*

The earth is doing a lot more than just rotating, but the result of the rotation just happens to be the most apparent to us every 24 hours…as day follows night. The earth also orbits around the sun once a year traveling at about 67,000 miles per hour…a distance of about 940 million kilometers. The earth also moves *with* the sun around the center of our galaxy…and moves *with* our galaxy out into intergalactic space!!!

During the entire time that the earth is rotating, orbiting, and traveling along on its journey through space, the earth maintains a constant *23º axis tilt.* This *tilt* is significant as it affects the seasons and climates of the earth because of which parts are closer and which parts are farther away from the sun. When the earth tilts closer to the sun the seasons will be summer/spring and warm climate. When the earth is tilted away from the sun the seasons will be fall/winter and cooler climate. So here's a question for the *nones: "What are the odds that our planet earth could maintain this 23° tilt as it travels through space at 67,000 miles per hour for 1000s of years…just by chance?"*

Gravity…God's Cosmic Glue

No discussion about this awesome planet that God created for us would be complete without discussing gravity—the thing that keeps us from flying off the earth. Without gravity the earth would explode into space. Gravity is the magnetic, mystifying force that directs the universe, with God's *creative* permission, of course! Gravity not only is the most pervasive force in the universe, but also it acts on *everything—particles, people, planets, stars, galaxies*—from the miniscule to the massive. Gravity binds our solar system together like cosmic glue, directing the stars, planets, and galaxies on their cosmic rollercoaster ride with prescribed precision. Gravity affects us 24-7, sleeping or standing. *Nothing* escapes its pull. Scientists have found that even the hearts, muscles, and bone density of astronauts show negative effects when deprived of gravity over long periods in space.

We've been discussing our planet earth as a part of the universe, but let's turn our attention now to some interesting *quick facts* just about the earth…

- The earth is the THIRD PLANET from the sun, and the densest and fifth-largest of the eight planets in the solar system.

- The SIZE of the earth at the equator is 7,926.41 miles.

- The earth WEIGHS 6,600,000,000,000,000,000,000 tons.

- The SURFACE AREA of the earth is 196,800,000 square miles.

- The CIRCUMFERENCE of the earth at the equator is 25,000 miles.

- The ATMOSPHERE COMPOSITION is 78% nitrogen, 1% oxygen, 1% argon, with other gases making up the remainder.

- The CRUST COMPOSITION is 46.6% oxygen, 27.7% silicon, 8.1% aluminum, 5% iron, 3.6% calcium, 2.8% sodium, 2.6% potassium, 2% magnesium, with other elements making up the remainder.

- The TEMPERATURE ranges from 136° F to 128.6° F.

- ONE DAY = 23 hours, 56 minutes, 4.09 seconds; we round to 24 hours.

- ONE YEAR = 365 days, 6 hours, 9 minutes, 9.54 seconds; we round to 365 days.

- 70% of the earth's surface is covered with WATER.

- The earth is the only planet in the solar system with PLATE TECTONICS which allows the earth to recycle its carbon...*otherwise the earth would overheat!*

- 75% of the earth's ATMOSPHERE is contained within the first 11 km above the earth's surface.

- DISTINCTIVE FEATURE: Earth is the only known planet that supports life.

- The earth's molten iron core turns it into A GIANT MAGNET, the magnetosphere extending out 1000s of kilometers above the earth, channeling the solar winds around the earth. This is important because without the protection of the MAGNETOSPHERE, the surface of the earth would be exposed to significant amounts of harmful radiation.

Try wrapping your *finite* mind around the insurmountable and *humanly impossible* task of designing a planet—including a sustainable ecosystem—that will accommodate all the needs of billions of plant and animal species *and* human beings that will inhabit the earth for 1000s of years! One only needs to take a glance at the facts about the earth listed earlier to conclude that *ONLY GOD COULD DESIGN SUCH A PERFECT PLANET.* He knew precisely how much SPACE would be needed...how much WATER...the right makeup of the ATMOSPHERE...how much OXYGEN...how much FOOD...the right amount of MINERALS, and a miscellany of NATURAL RESOURCES. Add to that the required physics and mathematical genius in designing and directing the universe. As the artist reveals himself in his painting, so God reveals Himself, His creative power and infinite genius in all that He has created.

The Rest of God's Third Day at Work

After God separated land from water on the earth, we read in Genesis 1:11 that God said, *"Let the land produce vegetation: seed-bearing plants and trees on the land that bear fruit with seed in it, according to their various*  *kinds."* Of course, the agnostics and atheists love to challenge the literal six days of creation by asking, how plants would be able to survive before the sun was created on the fourth day, since plants need the sun for photosynthesis to occur.

In response to this *pseudo* sequence-of-creation dilemma posed by the *nones*, Bible scholars and believers say this sequence of creation events actually reinforces the fact of a six-day creation. *"Light"* was supernaturally available via the Shekinah Glory of God's presence through His Son (the *light of the world)* during the creation process. (Genesis 1:3; Genesis 1:26) This creation sequence draws attention to the fact that God created everything (*by the word of His mouth*) as a completely- developed entity, negating the need for eons of time to pass while creations *"evolved."* Plants were created on day three, *fully formed.* They certainly could have survived for one day without the sun...even if one doubts that the Shekinah Glory provided the light needed for photosynthesis. Remember, the sun was created the next day.

Also noteworthy in Genesis 1:11, when God created the plants and trees, what He made was perfect *as created*— no need for changes. To make sure that His perfect designs would continue forever, he planted within them seeds that would replicate the original, and He designed a supportive ecosystem that would be ensure that His plan was sustainable. For example, all plants produce a flower at some point during the process of their growth. The flower itself produces seeds, which are then pollinated by either being transported by birds or insects, or by being released into the wind or dropped from the plant. Flowers help keep the ecosystem growing and providing for new plant life. Flowers also provide a food source for local insects and birds. In addition, certain bugs like bees produce honey from the nectar of the flowers, pollinating the flowers as they do so, thereby allowing the flowers to produce seeds. Without insects or birds to help in the pollinating process, flowers would have no way of reproducing or creating new flowers.

According to the Botanical Garden Conservation International, the number of plant species currently in existence is not clear. New species are still being identified, one researcher estimating that only 10% of existing flora had been discovered or identified. The most conservative number of known plant species is around 400,000…another example of God's infinite creativity and variety as a part of His perfect ecosystem.

Trees were also a part of God's third day at work and an extremely important part of earth's environment. There are about 20,000 species of trees in the world. Trees get an estimated 90% of their nutrition from the atmosphere and only 10% from the soil, and interestingly, no tree dies of old age. They generally are killed by insects, disease, or by people.

Some of the oldest trees have been known to live 4,000-5,000+ years. The oldest-known single-living tree was discovered in 2012 in the White Mountains of east central California. The Bristlecone Pine Tree pictured above is 5063 years old! The largest area of forest in the tropics remains the Amazon Basin, an estimated 81.5 million acres. Here are a few more quick facts about trees…

- An average size tree produces enough oxygen in one year to keep a family of four breathing.

- Three trees planted in the right place around buildings can cut air conditioning costs up to 50%.

- Trees generate jobs and contribute raw materials for buildings, newspapers, books, and more than 15,000 other forest products.

- Wood by-products become such products as vitamins, plastics, vanilla flavoring, photographic film, toothpaste, and medicines.

- By planting 20 million trees, the earth and its people will be provided with 260 million more tons of oxygen.

- Those same 20 million trees will remove 10 million tons of CO_2.

- Trees provide shelter and food for wildlife such as birds, squirrels, and bugs.

- Groves of trees provide food and cover for larger mammals, such as raccoons and deer.

- Trees make people feel good.

- Workers are more productive when they see trees along their commute routes and from their office windows.

- Hospital patients with a view of trees spend 8% fewer days in the hospital.

- Trees in the landscape relax us, lower heart rates, and reduce stress.

The vast variety of species of plants and trees and the design built into their reproduction and sustainability could be the result of *only* Divine plan. If that were not enough to change the doubting mind, in the following chapter, we will consider how God's hand is evident throughout the Bible from Genesis to Revelations as well as throughout all creation using mathematics of the highest order.

Chapter Six

God, the Master Mathematician

God created the whole system of mathematics all at once and vast beyond our comprehension. A part could not exist without the whole—no need for growth, change, improvement, or evolution, because it was perfect from the beginning. 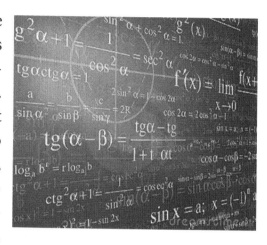 If one reasons by analogy, is it not reasonable to say that God who *flashed* upon the whole universe and the limitless system of mathematics in an *instant,* ALSO *spoke the world into existence* just as Moses says in the Genesis account? This same analogy also supports the doctrine of the creation of man *in a day* as well.

The vast system of mathematics which could not exist without a creator is so extensive that doctoral degrees are still being offered in universities. New subjects are added, new textbooks written, new formulas devised, new principles demonstrated. The *Author* of this fathomless science laughs at the *combined knowledge* of all the mathematicians of the past, present, and future.

We can learn a lot about how mathematics figured into God's perfect designs by looking at some math discovered in nature. Leonardo Pisano Fibonacci, an Italian number theorist born in Italy and educated in North Africa, was considered to be one of the most talented mathematicians of the Middle Ages. It was Fibonacci who gave us our decimal number system (Hindu-Arabic 0-9), the numbering system which replaced the Roman numeral system which had no 0's and lacked place value.

Fibonacci remains famous today for his Fibonacci numbers and Fibonacci sequence to solve math problems. The Sequence is 1, 1, 2, 3, 5, 8, 13, 21, 34, and 55, showing that each number is the sum of the two preceding numbers. This sequence is seen and used in many different areas of mathematics and science, and is an example of *recursive sequence.* Fibonacci numbers appear everywhere in nature, from the leaf arrangement in plants, to the pattern of the florets of a flower, the bracts of a pinecone, and the scales of a pineapple. The Fibonacci numbers are therefore applicable to the growth of every living thing, including a single cell, a grain of wheat, a hive of bees, and even all of mankind!

Fibonacci numbers have been called Nature's numbering system; however, the Christian community takes issue with using the word, *"nature." Nature* is the term that *man* has ascribed to specific categories of things created. But *in the beginning,* many centuries before Fibonacci *discovered* the numbers in nature, it was *God who created and designed this numbering system...in nature!*

Many plants show the Fibonacci numbers in the arrangement of the leaves around the stem. Some pine cones and fir cones also show the numbers, as do daisies and sunflowers. Many other plants such as succulents show the numbers. Some coniferous trees show these numbers in the bumps  on their trunks, and palm trees show the numbers in the rings on their trunks. Leaves on some plants are staggered in a spiral pattern to permit optimum exposure to sunlight. In the case of close-packed leaves in cabbages and succulents, the correct arrangement may be crucial for availability of space. For whatever reason, we can be confident that God had a purpose in everything He designed.

Mathematics in the Bible

As long as we're on the subject of numbers, let me deviate for a moment to discuss the evidence coming from mathematical patterns and numeric designs in the Bible which overwhelms the *finite* mind. The Bible has many unique properties revealing its Divine origin, but one of the most amazing is that it was written with a "sevenfold mathematical structure and design" hidden within the Hebrew and Greek languages in which it was written. The number seven, or an exact multiple of seven, repeatedly figures in every conceivable way from Genesis through Revelation.

The Bible, which is the world's number one best seller, is not strictly one book. In fact, it is a composite of 66 books written over 1500 years by about 40 different authors. All authors state that they are describing and recording visions, commandments and information inspired to them by God and that He is the ultimate *Author* behind what they have written. A sevenfold mathematical pattern permeates scripture showing clearly that it is indeed the product of "supernatural engineering" rather than mere human thought. It is something so complicated that no human composer could have achieved it. The Holy Bible bears the indisputable signature of God.

Look at Genesis 1:1: "In the beginning God created the heavens and the earth." The number of Hebrew words in this proclamation is seven. The total numerical value of the three nouns, God, heaven, and earth, is 777, a figure exactly divisible by seven. The number of letters in these three nouns is 14, exactly divisible by seven. The numerical value of the verb "created" is 203, exactly divisible by seven. The numerical value of the first and last letters of the seven words of this proclamation is 1393, exactly divisible by seven. The total number of Hebrew letters in these seven words is 28, exactly divisible by seven. And so it goes on. In this proclamation alone, linguists have identified a total of 18 separate features of the number seven.

This sevenfold structure or pattern is found throughout Scripture and is completely unique to the Bible. The number seven underlies and permeates the text in every conceivable manner. These patterns aren't found in any other ancient literature. Matthew, Mark, Luke, John, and all the other writings of John including Revelation, James, Peter, Jude, and all the writings of St. Paul display these phenomena as do all the writings of the Old Testament.

It has also been noted that the numeric value of the Hebrew names of the 21 Old Testament writers is exactly divisible by seven. Of these 21 writers, those names in the New Testament are Moses, David, Isaiah, Jeremiah, Daniel, Hosea, and Joel, in all exactly seven. The numeric value of these seven names is exactly divisible by seven. These seven names occur in the Old Testament 2,310 times, again a number exactly divisible by seven. The examples never seem to come to an end. This sevenfold pattern in Scripture interlocks paragraph with paragraph and book with book throughout the entire Bible.

I should state here that the founding father of the Science of Bible Numerics was a Russian mathematician and literary scholar, Dr. Ivan Panin. This mathematician and analytical genius grew up an ardent atheist! But after entering Harvard University, his conversion from atheism to Christianity made newspaper headlines. One day after his conversion, he was casually reading St. John's gospel in Greek and noticed what appeared to be a numerical relationship between certain words. Dr. Panin devoted the next 50 years of his life exploring and highlighting the numerical designs in the Greek New Testament texts and the Hebrew Old Testament texts. During this time he produced over 43,000 pages of analysis showing the hand of God working behind the human authors of the Bible. The mathematical patterns he revealed have never been denied. You can't argue with God's mathematics!

Most importantly, Panin's research proved the supernatural origin of Scripture at the very same time liberal critics were becoming popular by casting doubts on the reliability of the Bible. Panin died in 1942, but the research he began continues to this day. The Bible is no work of mere human origin but the work of God the Holy Spirit as seen in the following scriptures...

"Holy men of God spoke as they were moved by the Holy Spirit." 2 Peter 1:21

"All scripture is given by the inspiration of God." 2 Timothy 3:16

For one last example, take the genealogy of Jesus, the Son of God, as recorded in the first eleven verses of Matthew's Gospel. Studying the passage as it was written in New Testament Greek, research reveals the following amazing details:

- The number of the entire genealogy is exactly divisible by seven.

- The number of letters used is exactly divisible by seven.

- The number of words that begin with a vowel is exactly divisible by seven.

- The number of words that begin with a consonant is exactly divisible by seven.

- The number of words that occur more than once is exactly divisible by seven.

- The number of words that occur in more than one form is exactly divisible by seven.

- The number of words that occur in only one form is exactly divisible by seven.

- The number of nouns is exactly divisible by seven.

- Only seven words are not nouns.

- The number of names in the genealogy is exactly divisible by seven.

- Only seven other kinds of nouns occur.

- The number of male names is exactly divisible by seven.

- The number of generations is 21, exactly divisible by seven.

- The mathematical structure observed in the genealogy of Jesus is staggering, showing clearly that this couldn't be the work of *unaided* human thought, but only the result of *Divine* inspiration!

God's numerical accuracy is also observed in the hatching of eggs. For example: The eggs of the potato bug hatch in 7 days; eggs of the canary in 14 days; eggs of the barnyard hen in 21 days; eggs of ducks and geese in 28 days; eggs of the mallard in 35 days; eggs of the parrot and ostrich in 42 days...*all divisible by seven!*

God's mathematical designs are revealed in His arrangement, sections, and segments of various foods He created. For example: Each watermelon has an even number of stripes on the rind; each orange has an even number of segments; each ear of corn has an even number of rows; each stalk of wheat has an even number of grains; every bunch of bananas has on its lowest row an even number of bananas, and each row decreases by one, so that the one row has an even number and the next row an odd number. What's more, God's math includes precise and detailed record-keeping skills, even about seemingly less-important matters...

"Indeed the very hairs of your head are all numbered."
Luke 12:7a

Chapter Seven

Prophecy as Proof

In the last chapter, we were exploring Mathematics and the Bible. Did you know that in Jesus' life, he fulfilled 332 distinct prophecies from the Old Testament—according to Max Lucado, pastor and bestselling author on p. 373, *Grace for the Moment, Vol. 2.* The mathematical *"improbability"* is staggering of that many prophecies being fulfilled in the life of *one* man. Max already did the calculations for you, and the answer has a lot of zeroes. The *unlikely* chances are…one in

840,000,000,000,000,000,000,000,000,000,

000,000,000,000,000,000,000,000,000,000,

000,000,000,000,000,000,000,000,000,000,0

(That's 840, followed by 97 zeroes!)

As more and more evidence of the Bible's accuracy is unearthed, it is being reconsidered as not only a historical document and a reliable map for archaeological discovery, but also as a collection of instructions for human living.

If you'd like to check out *some* of the Old Testament prophecies that were literally fulfilled by Jesus of Nazareth for yourself, see the Messianic Prophecies Chart that follows...

Prophecies Concerning His Birth	Prophecy	Fulfillment
Born of the Seed of Woman	GEN 3:15	GAL 4:4
Born of a Virgin	ISA 7:14	MAT 1:18; MAT 1:24-25
Son of God	PSA 2:7	MAT 3:17
Seed of Abraham	GEN 22:18	MAT 1:1
Son of Isaac	GEN 21:12	LUK 3:23; LUK 3:34
Tribe of Judah	GEN 49:10	LUK 3:23; LUK 3:33

Family Line of Jesse	ISA 11:1	LUK 3:23; LUK 3:32
House of David	JER 23:5	LUK 3:23; LUK 3:31
Born at Bethlehem	MIC 5:2	MAT 2:1
Presented with Gifts	PSA 72:10	MAT 2:1; MAT 2:11
Herod Kills Children	JER 31:15	MAT 2:16
Prophecies Concerning His Nature	**Prophecy**	**Fulfillment**
His Pre-Existence	MIC 5:2	COL 1:17; JOH 17:5
He Shall Be Called Lord	PSA 110:1	MAT 22:43-45
Shall Be Immanuel	ISA 7:14	MAT 1:23
Shall Be a Prophet	DEU 18:18	MAT 21:11
Priest	PSA 110:4	HEB 3:1
Judge	ISA 33:22	JOH 5:30
King	PSA 2:6	MAT 27:37

Special Anointing of Holy Spirit	ISA 11:2	MAT 3:16-17
His Zeal for God	PSA 69:9	JOH 2:15-16
Prophecies Concerning His Ministry	**Prophecy**	**Fulfillment**
Preceded by a Messenger	ISA 40:3	MAT 3:1-2
Ministry Began in Galilee	ISA 9:1	MAT 4:12; MAT 4:13; MAT 4:17
Ministry of Miracles	ISA 35:5-6	MAT 9:35
Teacher of Parables	PSA 78:2	MAT 13:34
He Was to Enter the Temple	MAL 3:1	MAT 21:12
He Was to Enter Jerusalem on a Donkey	ZEC 9:9	LUK 19:35-37
Stone of Stumbling to Jews	PSA 118:22	1PE 2:7
Light to Gentiles	ISA 60:3	ACT 13:47-48

Prophecies Concerning Events After His Burial	Prophecy	Fulfillment
Resurrection	PSA 16:10	ACT 2:31
Ascension	PSA 68:18	ACT 1:9
Session	PSA 110:1	HEB 1:3
Prophecies Fulfilled in One Day	Prophecy	Fulfillment
Betrayed by a Friend	PSA 41:9	MAT 10:4
Sold For 30 Pieces of Silver	ZEC 11:12	MAT 26:15
Money to Be Thrown into God's House	ZEC 11:13	MAT 27:5
Price Given for Potter's Field	ZEC 11:13	MAT 27:7
Forsaken by His Disciples	ZEC 13:7	MAR 14:50
Accused By False Witnesses	PSA 35:11	MAT 26:59-60
Silent Before Accusers	ISA 53:7	MAT 27:12
Wounded and Bruised	ISA 53:5	MAT 27:26
Smitten and Spit Upon	ISA 50:6	MAT 26:67

Mocked	PSA 22:7-8	MAT 27:29
Fell Under the Cross	PSA 109:24-25	JOH 19:17
Hands and Feet Pierced	PSA 22:16	LUK 23:33
Crucified with Thieves	ISA 53:12	MAT 27:38
Prophecies Fulfilled in One Day (Continued)	**Prophecy**	**Fulfillment**
Crucified with Thieves	ISA 53:12	MAT 27:38
Made Intercession for His Persecutors	ISA 53:12	LUK 23:34
Rejected By His Own Countrymen	ISA 53:3	JOH 7:5; JOH 7:48
Hated Without a Cause	PSA 69:4	JOH 15:25
Friends Stood Afar Off	PSA 38:11	LUK 23:49
People Shook Their Heads	PSA 109:25	MAT 27:39
Stared Upon	PSA 22:17	LUK 23:35
Garments Parted and Lots Cast	PSA 22:18	JOH 19:23-24
To Suffer Thirst	PSA 69:21	JOH 19:28

Gall and Vinegar Offered to Him	PSA 69:21	MAT 27:34
His Forsaken Cry	PSA 22:1	MAT 27:46
Committed Himself to God	PSA 31:5	LUK 23:46
Bones Not Broken	PSA 34:20	JOH 19:33
Heartbroken	PSA 22:14	JOH 19:34
His Side Pierced	ZEC 12:10	JOH 19:34
Darkness Over the Land	AMO 8:9	MAT 27:45
Buried in a Rich Man's Tomb	ISA 53:9	MAT 27:57-60

Chapter Eight

Foreknowledge of God

"All Scripture is God-breathed and useful for teaching,
rebuking, correcting and training in righteousness."
2 Timothy 3:16

The Bible is the *only* book that can boast that it's written by a *supernatural Author!* God declares boldly in His Word that He alone can accurately predict the future and challenges false prophets from other religions to prove otherwise. (Isaiah 46:8-11; Isaiah 41:21-24) Let's look at twenty *quick facts* (selected and condensed from Christsavesministries.org) that prove that this statement is true.

1. *Fact:* THE BIBLE CONTAINS 66 BOOKS, penned by about 40 different and *inspired* writers, over 1000's of years, yet maintains totally cohesive design.

2. *Fact:* OVER 332 FULFILLED PROPHECIES from the Old Testament concerning the birth, life, and death of Jesus Christ.

3. *Fact:* Genesis 1:9 stated over 3400 years ago that THE WHOLE EARTH WAS COVERED WITH WATER. Evidence from modern science now recognizes this fact.

4. *Fact:* Genesis 1:14-16 lists THE PURPOSE OF THE SUN, MOON, and STARS as *signs, seasons, days, and years.* Science caught up thousands of years later using powerful telescopes.

5. *Prophecy:* In Genesis 1:27-28, we read that GOD CREATED MAN AND GAVE HIM DOMINION over all other living creatures on the earth. 3400 years later, man still has dominion over all species of all kinds in the world.

6. *Fact:* In Genesis 2:7, (3500 years ago) GOD FORMED MAN FROM DUST *from the ground.* Modern science confirms that the basic elements of man's body is composed of sixteen elements: carbon, hydrogen, nitrogen, oxygen, fluorine, sodium, magnesium, silicon, sulfur, phosphorus, chlorine, potassium, calcium, manganese, iron, and iodine—all found in the dust of the ground!

7. *Prophecy:* In Genesis 3:16, the BIBLE PROMISES A CURSE UPON WOMAN *multiplying her pain in child bearing.* With all the advances in modern medicine 3500 years later, women still experience great pain in childbearing.

8. *Prophecy:* In Genesis 3:19, MEN WERE CURSED RELATED TO EARNING A LIVING. 3400 years later, men still struggle to provide for themselves and their families.

9. *Prophecy:* In Genesis 15:5, GOD PROMISED ABRAHAM THAT HIS DESCENDANTS WOULD BE WITHOUT NUMBER *just as the stars are without number.* 3400 years later, science confirms that in our Milky Way *alone*, there are over 200 billion stars!

10. *Fact:* In Isaiah 40:22, (2700 years ago) THE BIBLE TOLD US THE EARTH IS ROUND, despite the fact most ancient scientists believed the earth was flat. It wasn't until 1519-1521 that Magellan proved the earth to be round.

11. *Fact:* In Job 26:7, (3400 years ago) THE BIBLE STATES THE EARTH WAS SUSPENDED IN SPACE, contrary to what ancient scientists believed—that the earth was supported on the backs of elephants, turtles, or serpents!

12. *Fact:* In Luke 17:34-36, (2000 years ago) speaking of his second coming, JESUS WAS AWARE OF DAYTIME AND NIGHTTIME—*AT THE SAME TIME*—ON DIFFERENT PARTS OF THE EARTH. This *foreknowledge* was before man even knew the earth was round, much less that one side of the earth was day, the other night!

13. *Fact:* In Ecclesiastes 1:6, 2000 years ago, THE BIBLE DESCRIBES THE LAWS OF METEOROLOGY, before science had any ideas about predicting weather or climate changes.

14. *Fact:* In Psalm 135:7 and Job 36:27, (written 3400 years ago) we learn that GOD DESIGNED THE SOURCE OF RAIN *from the ends of the earth.* Science didn't know that rain water came from *evaporation* until 1888 when a German scientist discovered the basic laws of aerodynamics, thermodynamics, and hydrodynamics.

15. *Fact:* In Job 38:30 and Psalm 147:15-17, (3000 years ago) we learn that GOD COMMANDS THE WEATHER EVENTS OF THE EARTH…from *frozen sea water* to *quick-freezing the earth.* Science didn't learn that large bodies of water could be frozen until the 17th century when Henry Hudson explored the arctic regions of the North Pole. And Since 1806, quick-frozen carcasses of mammoths have been found, their flesh still fresh enough to eat!

16. *Fact:* In Genesis 11:7-9, we learn that GOD CONFUSED THE LANGUAGES OF THE EARTH. A *minimal* estimate of some 2500-3000 ideo-ethnic languages exist in the world. This prophecy still prevents a one-world nation because of language diversity.

17. *Prophecy:* In Revelation 13:16-17, (2000 years ago) THE BIBLE PROPHESIED MAN WILL NOT BE ABLE TO BUY OR SELL—*without a mark on his arm or head,* a

strange prediction before technology existed for marking every member of the human race! Today we do have technology for implanting chips under people's skin, even in their brains.

18. *Prophecy:* In Micah 5:2, JEWISH PROPHETS WROTE THAT THE MESSIAH WOULD BE BORN IN BETHLEHEM. In Matthew 2:1, this prophecy was fulfilled…700 years later!

19. *Prophecy:* In Psalm 22:16, we find THE PROPHECY OF THE CRUCIFIXION OF JESUS. Note: The Book of Psalms was written more than 1000 years before the time of Jesus, and crucifixion was not known to exist when the Book of Psalms was written!

20. *Prophecy:* In Psalm 16:10 (1440 BC) we find PROPHECY OF THE RESURRECTION OF CHRIST from the grave; in Psalm 68:18 (1440 BC) PROPHECY OF THE ASCENSION OF CHRIST INTO HEAVEN; and in Hosea 6:2 (715 BC) we find the PROPHECY OF CHRIST'S RESURRECTION AFTER THREE DAYS!

Billy Graham says the Bible continues to be the only *eternally-contemporary book* answering universal, human-heart questions that haven't changed over the centuries—*Who am I, Why am I here, Where did I come from, Where am I going when I die, and How should I live?*

Chapter Nine

Day Four: Two Great Lights

"And God made the two great lights; the greater light to rule the day, and the lesser light to rule the night: He made the stars also. And God set them in the firmament of heaven to give light upon the earth, and to rule over the day and over the night, and to divide the light from the darkness: and God saw that it was good. And there was evening and there was morning, a fourth day." Genesis 1:16-19

The Biblical assertion is that God spoke, and all things came into existence. (Hebrews 11:3) The obvious question is, why is it so hard to believe that it was *days* of creation, just as the scriptures state? The answer: because belief in a Creator God requires *faith*, not just science. The Bible teaches that everything God created was complete and mature...*instantly.* So, why is it so far-fetched to believe that the universe itself also was created with age, stability, or maturity? For example, the nearest star to Earth is Alpha Centauri, 4.3 million light years away. Stars must have

been made *functional;* otherwise man could not have seen and used them to gauge time—*for signs and seasons, for days and for years. (Genesis 1:14)*

One must assume that the stars along with other created things had to have had some kind of stability or maturity... *in the beginning...before* the second law of thermodynamics (entropy) entered and *age* began as a deteriorating factor. It's even more incredulous to believe that the universe is as old as claimed by progressive creationists because by their calculations we would have run out of heat a *long, long, long* time ago!

It's so much easier simply to take God at His word, from the One who was there at the beginning, and the One who *upholds the world in His hands.* (Hebrews 1:1-3) Jesus turned the water into wine without any *time-consuming* fermentation process. He created *MORE* fish from the few to feed 5000, and this *new fish largesse* had never seen an ocean! This Jesus also created organic miracles, making new eyes, and giving life to where there was none. Is there anything too hard for our Creator God?

For example: Our Sun has inspired mythology in almost all cultures, including ancient Egyptians, Aztecs, Native Americans, and Chinese. All living things on Earth are dependent on the Sun to stay alive. All life on Earth needs the Sun to thrive and grow. All energy that humans consume originates from the sun, either directly or indirectly. Plants need sunlight to grow. Humans need plants or animals that eat plants, in order to stay alive. Also, electricity is generated by burning oil or coal, which is essentially ancient plants.

While some electricity is created using solar or wind energy, it is still dependent on the Sun. Let's look at some quick sun facts and some Biblical *"Son"* analogies...

- Our Sun is actually a massive, shining sphere of hot gas, about 70% hydrogen and 28% helium. <u>Biblical Analogy</u>: *"He's the bright and morning star."* Revelation 22:16

- The Sun is by far the largest object in the Solar System and the closest star to the Earth. The Sun appears much larger than the other 100 billion stars in the Milky Way galaxy because it is so close to Earth. <u>Biblical Analogy</u>: *"I am the Lord, and there is no other; apart from me there is no God."* Isaiah 45:5

- Interaction between the Sun and the Earth drives the seasons, the currents in the ocean, the weather, and the climate.

- The Sun's gravitational pull holds Earth and the other planets in place, keeping the planets orbiting inside the Solar System. <u>Biblical Analogy</u>: *"And I, if I be lifted up from the earth, will draw all men unto me."* John 12:32

- If the Sun were to disappear, all plants and animals would eventually die. <u>Biblical Analogy</u>: *"Whoever has the Son has life; whoever does not have the Son does not have life."* 1 John 5:12

- The Sun is larger than all the planets with a radius of 432,000 miles. This is nearly 109 times the size of the

Earth. It is about 865,000 miles across. <u>Biblical Analogy</u>: *"God made two great lights—the greater light to govern the day and the lesser light to govern the night."* Genesis 1:16

- The Sun is incredibly hot, the outer part about 10,000 degrees Fahrenheit which is about 50 times hotter than the temperature at which water boils...so hot that all metals would be vaporized on the Sun.

- The surface of the Sun has lots of eruptions known as prominences or flames. Some of these larger flames are even bigger than the Earth.

- All planets in our Solar System revolve around the Sun...including the Earth, Mars, Venus, Saturn, and Jupiter. The length of time it takes a planet to revolve around the Sun is referred to as a year, 365 days in an Earth year. <u>Biblical Analogy</u>: *"And God said, "Let there be lights in the vault of the sky to separate the day from the night, and let them serve as signs to mark sacred times, and days and years."* Genesis 1:14

- It takes 8.3 minutes for light from the Sun to reach the Earth. <u>Biblical Analogy</u>: Our prayers reach the SON instantly...no call waiting or busy signals..."*Call to me and I will answer you and tell you great and unsearchable things you do not know."* Jeremiah 33:3

The Moon, the *Lesser* Light

How often have you walked barefoot on the beach and watched while the white-crested waves slap the shoreline

with rhythmic regu-
larity, regardless of the
weather? Makes one
wonder how many bil-
lions of times this God-
driven phenomenon has
repeated itself since time
began.

The gravity of the Moon (and to a lesser degree, the Sun) and the rotation of the earth cause the tides in Earth's oceans. The simplest explanation is that as the Earth spins, the Moon's grav-ity tugs at the ocean under it, causing it to bulge out. This bulge is the *high tide,* and as the Earth rotates on its axis, the bulge sweeps around the Earth. The movement of the Moon in its orbit causes the timing of the *high tides* to shift slightly each day.

Here are just a few quick facts about the Moon…

- The Moon shows only one face to the earth and is the 5th largest natural satellite in the Solar System.

- Only 12 people have ever stepped onto the surface of the Moon, but NASA plans to return humans to the Moon to set up a permanent research station in 2019.

- The Earth's gravity holds the Moon in its orbit, but it pulls differently at various parts of the moon.

- From our perspective here on Earth, the Moon appears to be the same size as the Sun, but the Sun is 400 times larger than the Moon and 400 times further away.

- The tides on earth are caused mostly by the gravitational pull of the Moon, but the Sun also helps pull the earth's water. That's why we get very high and low tides from time to time. When the gravity of the Moon and the Sun are in line, we have the biggest and also the smallest tides.

- Gravity on the Moon is 17% of that on the Earth.

Chapter Ten

Day Five: Fish and Birds

*"Let the waters abound with an abundance of living
creatures, and let the birds fly above the earth across
the face of the firmament of the heavens."*
Genesis 1:20

Before we get to Marine Life and Birds, we must look for a moment at the Creator's environmental plan and design of wind and waves and the effects on oceanography. Waves have a major influence on the marine environment and ultimately on the planet's climate. Waves travel effortlessly along the water's surface, made possible by small movements of the water molecules. The wind blows over the water, changing its surface into ripples and waves. As the waves grow in height, the wind pushes them along faster and higher. Waves can become unexpectedly strong and destructive. In the real world, waves do not have idealized, harmonious shape, but irregular. They are composed of several interfering waves of different frequency and speed. But as waves enter shallow water, they become taller and slow down, eventually breaking on the shore.

Without waves, the world would be a much different place. We know that waves cannot exist by themselves, they are caused by winds. Winds in turn are caused by differences in temperature on the planet, mainly between the hot tropics and the cold poles, but also due to the temperature fluctuations of continents relative to the sea. Without waves, the winds would have only a very small grip on the water and not able to move it as much. The waves allow the wind to transfer its energy to the water's surface and make it move.

At the surface, waves then promote the exchange of gases—carbon dioxide into the ocean and oxygen out. Currents and eddies mix the layers of water which would otherwise become stagnant and less conducive to life. This cycle allows nutrients to be circulated and re-used...all according to God's purposeful plan.

Ocean currents allow the larvae of marine life to be dispersed and carried great distances. Many creatures spawn only during storms when large waves can mix their germ cells effectively. Coastal creatures living in shallow waters experience the brunt of the waves directly, so in order to survive they need to be robust and adaptable. Waves influence the biodiversity on creatures living at surface level down to depths of 30 meters or more. Without waves, there would not be as many species living in the sea. Waves also make beaches by transporting sand from deeper down toward the shore and by washing the sand. Waves stir and suspend the sand so that currents or gravity can transport it.

The scope of God's creative design and variety staggers the imagination once again as we examine the ecological structure of marine life! Ever wondered just how many fish species there are? After a just-published ten-year extensive study, The Census of Marine Life takes a stab at answering this question, estimating that there are more than 230,000 species living in our oceans! More than 360 scientists from around the world participated in this ten-year study, surveying 25 different regions from the Antartic through the more temperate and tropical seas, to the Artic, attempting a *head count* of the different kinds of marine plants and animals. The study which was carried out also covered animals such as crabs, plankton, birds, sponges, worms, squids, sharks, and slugs. The estimate for known fish species alone is 30,000, just a tiny example of God's limitless creativity!

The results of the study found that just about 20% of the marine species of the world are crustaceans such as lobsters, krill, barnacles, and crabs. If we toss in Mollusks (such as squid and octopus) and fish (which include sharks), that adds up to about half of the number of species which we find in the oceans of the world. The more charismatic species—sea lions, turtles, whales, and sea birds—make up less than 2% of all the species in our world's oceans.

Not only do we see beauty and diversity in God's marine-life creativity, but also strategic planning. He provided an ecologically-refined, important, abundant, inexpensive, and accessible food resource for man from the beginning of creation to the present day. There's wisdom in the saying, *"Teach a man to fish, and you provide him with food for life!"*

A Few of God's Unique Marine-Life Creatures...

Mola Mola – The size of a fish is directly proportional to its container or environment as well as its ecological niche within that environment. Ocean Sunfish or Mola Mola, weighing up to 2200 pounds, are the heaviest bony-fish in the world!

Colossal Squid – The eye of the Colossal Squid is the largest animal eye known—about 27 cm across—about the size of a soccer ball. The Colossal Squid also has light organs—one on each eyeball. The squid uses these light organs like *headlights*, allowing him to see and catch prey, watch for predators, and see each other in the dark depths of the ocean. The Colossal Squid's eyes are positioned so that they face forward, giving him binocular or stereoscopic vision so he can judge the distance his tentacles need to move in order to strike and grab prey.

Scallops – Along with clams, oysters, and mussels, Scallops are classified as bivalves—animals that have two hinged shells. Unlike other bivalves, scallops can swim by clapping their shells quickly, moving a jet of water past the shell hinge which propels the scallop forward.

Scallops can have up to 100 eyes, and their beautiful "blue peepers" are not just there for looks. Scallops can see objects, as well as sense movement. Marine biologists equate their visual acuity with that of honeybees.

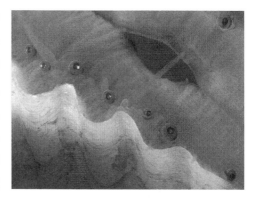

Octopus – There are about 300 species of Octopuses alone. They have two eyes and four pairs of arms that usually bear suction cups. They also have 3 hearts and 2 gills. They have a hard beak, with its mouth at the center point of the arms.

They do not have a skeleton which enables them to squeeze through tight places.

Octopuses trail along behind their eight arms as they swim. Their habitat is Coral reefs, open waters, and the ocean floor. Their weight is about 33 pounds with an arm span of from 4 to 14 feet. For small species, their lifespan is usually short—about 6 months, whereas Giant Octopuses live up to 5 years. Their diet consists of crabs, scallops, fish turtles, and crustaceans.

All Octopuses are venomous! The Blue-ringed Octopuses are deadly to humans, considered to be one of the world's most venomous creatures. One bite can completely paralyze and kill an adult.

Octopuses are intelligent, have excellent memories and also are trainable. Their main form of defense is to hide and camouflage—ejecting a cloud of blackish ink to escape from predators. They also have very good eyesight and sense of touch, but limited hearing.

The Black-Eyed Dragon Fish – This fish is found to have some remarkable abilities. Living at depths of 1500-4500 feet, the only light that gets through the water is a dim blue light. Sighted creatures that live at this depth are able to see well in this dim blue light, but none of them can see light in the red

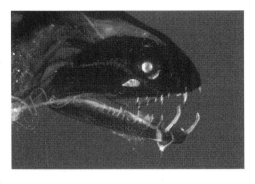

end of the spectrum, that is, none but the Dragon Fish, and *that's his secret weapon.* The Dragon Fish is the only known creature to have chlorophyll in its eyes, giving him the ability to see red light in the depths. *He makes his own red light which is invisible to his prey.* The Dragon Fish sees its red light reflecting off nearby prey, just like a sniper uses an infrared scope to sight prey in the dark.

The Dragon Fish's sniper-like ability to find its prey with light invisible to its prey *offers a powerful set of arguments in support of a Creator.* Its unique ability to see red where there is no red also bears powerful witness to an indescribably-wise Designer!

<u>Whales</u> – There are approximately 80 different species of whales coming in many shapes and sizes. The Whale Shark has over 4000 teeth, yet each tooth is only 3mm long. The Blue Whale's whistle is the loudest noise made by an animal, and his heart is the size of a small car. Humpback Whales create the loudest sound of any living creature!

Stonefish – Stonefish live off the coast of Australia and _are the most poisonous fish in the world!_ Its name reflects its ability to camouflage itself with the help of its grey and mottled coloring similar to a stone. For this reason swimmers inadvertently step on them, often leading to fatal situations. The Stone Fish have glands at the base of its 13 needle-like dorsal-fin spines, emitting toxins when it feels threatened or disturbed. Depending on the depth of the penetration of its poisonous spines, the poison takes as little as 2 hours to kill a human.

Sailfish – Although it's difficult to measure how fast a particular fish swims, the speed of the Sailfish has been estimated at faster than a sprinting Cheetah and up to 109 km/h. Its predatory behavior and body structure demonstrate God designed it for speed. Its rapier-like bill has been compared to the nose of a jet causing low-resistance flow. It also has a strong backbone and a sturdy crescent-shaped tail to complete the sprinting swimmer's body.

And Let the Birds Fly Above the Heavens...

> *"Look at the birds of the air, that they do not sow, nor reap nor gather into barns, and yet your heavenly Father feeds them. Are you not worth much more than they?* Matthew 6:26

A Few Facts about God's Fascinating Feathered Creations

There are about 10,000 living species of birds, and birds can be found on every continent. Birds are feathered, winged, and have two feet—the only exception is the wingless Kiwi bird of New Zealand. Birds communicate using visual signals, *unique* calls, and through songs. Ask the agnostic who taught the *first* Robin its song?

Birds' feathers are used to facilitate flight, provide insulation, for display and camouflage, and for signaling. The diet of birds can include fruit, plants, seeds, carrion, and various small animals including other birds. Most all birds fly, and their bones are hollow and thin-walled making them lighter for flight. Seventy-five percent of all wild birds die before they are six months old.

Pigeons – Their average flying speed over moderate distances is around 80 km/h (50 miles per hour) but speeds of up to 140 km/h (90 miles per hour) have been observed in top racers for short distances. The homing pigeon is selectively bred to find its

way home over extremely long distances. The wild rock pigeon has an innate homing ability, meaning that it will generally return to its nest and mate. This made it relatively easy to breed from the birds that repeatedly found their way home over long distances. Flights as long as 1,800 km (1,100 miles) have been recorded by birds in competitive pigeon racing. Homing pigeons were used in many places in the world and in wars and are called messenger or carrier pigeons when used for this purpose.

Penguins / Ostriches – Both of these are birds, but they do not fly. There are 17-20 species of Penguins, all of which live in the southern half of the globe. Most swim under water, and some reach speeds of 22 mph. Penguins' *"tuxedos"* are not fashion statements, but rather camouflage that help them to avoid predators. Like other birds, Penguins don't have teeth; they have backward-facing fleshy spines lining the inside of their mouths that help guide fleshy fish meals down their throat. During the summer, they eat about 2 pounds of seafood each day; in the winter, they eat 1/3 of that.

Eating so much seafood means they take in a lot of saltwater, so God designed Penguins with a *supraorbital gland* just behind the eye to filter the salt from their bloodstream. Penguins also hydrate themselves with meltwater and snow. God gave them another waterproofing oil gland that they spread across their feathers to insulate their bodies and reduce friction as they glide through the water. Feathers are quite important to Penguins living around Antarctica. Emperor Penguins have the highest density of any bird—100 feathers per square inch. These specially-designed glands and dense feathering of the Penguins definitely...*were not just by chance!*

The Ostrich lives in South Africa, is the largest of all birds, and produces the largest eggs, weighing about 3 pounds. They weigh up to 400 pounds, growing up to 10 feet tall. Ostriches also have the  largest eyes of any land animal. They are the fastest bird, and their running speed is more than 40 mph...covering up to 16 feet in a single stride.

They chase their prey in an awkward zigzag pattern, and the kick of an Ostrich can kill a lion! Ostriches are omnivores, chowing down on whatever is available. Ostriches can eat things other animals can't digest because their intestines are especially long and tough. They also have a gizzard, which, along with the stones and sand they swallow, helps grind up the food they eat. God's perfect environment left nothing to chance or need for revision. Even the Ostrich was part of His *food left-overs disposal team.*

Hummingbird – The Hummingbird is truly a marvel of God's creativity. One of the most fascinating and unique creatures of all creation is the common Hummingbird. What is the probability that all of the unique characteristics of the Ruby-Throated Hummingbird—each of which are needed for its survival—were developed by some step-by-step evolutionary process? A few of the Hummingbird's incredible abilities are listed below...

- Hummingbirds have brilliant iridescent plumage, long slender bills, and a life span of 3-5 years.

- They are tiny and can fit into the palm of your hand, approximately only two inches in length.

- A hummingbird heart weighs but a fraction of an ounce, but beats 800 times a minute!

- Their wings are specifically designed for vibrating flight, and when they beat their wings rapidly they produce a humming sound...hence their name.

- God designed the *helicopter-like* hummingbird with the unique ability to fly forward, backward, upside-down, and straight up; incidentally, no other bird can fly straight up or backward. *It was not until 1940, that man was able to build the first one-rotor helicopter!*

- They have a special fringed tongue to sweep insects out from the inside of flowers. It cannot survive on nectar alone, but also needs protein from eating insects. Without this special tongue it could never catch the insects.

- They can fly 500 miles nonstop over the Gulf waters to Mexico. The Hummingbird conserves its strength for long flights by taking a prolonged rest just prior to the flight and making every motion count in flight.

- They go into a "torpid" condition at night by almost shutting down their metabolism. Because of its incredibly high-energy activity, gram for gram, the Hummingbird has the greatest energy output of any warm-blooded animal. Yet at night, it uses only one-fifth of its normal energy.

- The Green Violet-Ear Hummingbird is one of the world's fastest birds, flying up to 150 kilometers per hour, beating their wings 80 times per second!

Woodpecker – There are over 200 species of Woodpeckers found all over the globe except in Australia, New Zealand, and Madagascar. They mate for life, have strong claws, short legs, and very pointed chisel-like bills for boring into wood for insects. They also have a stiff tail that facilitates climbing vertically up a tree trunk. Their heads are like shock absorbers, tapping 20 times per second, up to an estimated 12,000 times a day—without feeling pain—thanks to special (God-designed) air pockets in the skull. God also gave them bristle-like feathers on the nostrils to prevent inhalation of wood particles.

Bald Eagles – The Bald Eagle is one of the large birds of prey found in North America, second in size only to the California Condor. They have a choc-olate-brown body, a wing span of about 7 feet, a white head, and bright yellow bill and legs. The Bald Eagle is found near large bodies of open water with an abundant supply of trees for nesting. They have excellent eyesight; the frontal set-ting of their eyes gives them excellent binocular and periph-eral vision. They are powerful fliers, reaching speeds over 35 mph during level flight, and 75-100 mph in a hunting dive. Here are a few more interesting facts about Bald Eagles…

- Their longevity record is 28 years in the wild; 36 years in captivity.

- Bald Eagles have 7000 feathers and can fly to an altitude of 10,000 feet.

- The Bald Eagle's diet consists of fish, especially salmon and trout, but also eat rodents, snakes, carrion, and small animals.

- They are monogamous and mate for life.

- Adult Bald Eagles weigh 8-14 pounds.

- It has the distinction of being represented in the coat of arms, and on the coins of the United States, and is the national bird of America.

Chapter Eleven

Day Six: (Part A.) Animals and God's Life Boat

"And God made the beasts of the earth after their
kind, and the cattle after their kind, and everything
that creepeth upon the ground after its kind: and
God saw that it was good."
Genesis 1:25

"And God created man in his own image, in the image of
God created he him; male and female created he them."
Genesis 1:27

There are about 1,250,000 <u>identified</u> animal species. This number includes 1,190,200 invertebrates—among them 950,000 insects, 70,000 mollusks, 40,000 crustaceans, and 130,200 others. There are approximately 58,800 identified vertebrates, including 29,300 fish, 5,743 amphibians, 8,240 reptiles, 9,800 birds, and 5,416 mammals. By comparison, 300,000 plant species are known.

It is important to note that these numbers do not account for species which have not been captured or described scientifically. Scientists estimate that there may be as many as 10 to 30 million unidentified insect species and up to 1 million *mite species*—small anthropods, a related-animal group but not the same as insects.

Modern science is not aware of all the species on the planet. In the mid-18th century, when Carl Linnaeus and his pupils set out to record all the known species, they found only 15,000 species of animal. Today total-species estimates range from 2 to 30 million! In addition to all the species of animal, there are between 10 million and 1 billion species of bacteria and archaea.

Earth's biodiversity is much more than beauty and wonder; it underpins our ecosystem that sustains life on earth. Here's an FYI: It's estimated that in order to complete the inventory of all of Earth's remaining species could require up to 1,200 years of work by more than 300,000 taxonomists!

The only parts of Genesis that some people don't believe are the first eleven chapters. The rest of Genesis is pretty much universally accepted as factual and historic. The first eleven chapters are *suspect* because the *nones* believe that the world is millions of years old.

Evolutionists believe the world is millions of years old based upon the fossil record as a record of millions of years of evolution. Contrarily, Christians (and Creationists) accept the Biblical account of the flood, believing that the fossil record is a *record of a world-wide flood.* The Creationists offer the following explanation as proof. Floods do a lot of damage. A world-wide flood would bury all the animals *not on the ark!* At the time of the flood, the Bible says that *the fountains of the deep burst open.* This means that water and mud spewed forcefully out of the ground. Creationists believe this action is what caused the mid-Atlantic ridge and the shapes of the continents. The water whooshing back and forth with the tides for a year would create layers of sediment of different densities. This is why the sides of a canyon show layers. Animals that just die will rot or be eaten. An animal needs to be covered quickly to fossilize…the mineral replacing the live bone matter. Therefore, the fossil record really is a record of a massive world-wide flood.

God's "Life" Boat

I have to admit that even before I learned of the vast number of species of animals that God created, I wondered how they could have all gotten aboard Noah's Ark. For the things I didn't understand as I read the Bible, I just added them to my a*sk-God-when-I-get-to-Heaven* list. But when I began doing my research for this section, I found lots of answers…many right there in the Biblical account. For example, I learned that when God gave Noah the *blueprint* for the Ark to preserve His creations of animals and man, He knew exactly what size boat was needed.

"Make yourself an ark of gopherwood; make rooms in the ark, and cover it inside and outside with pitch. And this is how you shall make it: The length of the ark shall be 300 cubits, its width 50 cubits, and its height 30 cubits. You shall make a window for the ark, and you shall finish it to a cubit from above; and set the door of the ark in its side. You shall make it with lower, second, and third decks." Genesis 6:14-16

Answers for Some Anticipated Questions

How the Animals Had Room on Noah's Ark

In light of some one million species of animals, it's logical to doubt whether adequate space existed on the ark to accommodate all the animals. In reality, there are not really that many *kinds* of animals. God created the *basic types* or *kinds* of plants and animals, and then allowed genetic variation from the basic types. For example, God created the basic types of birds, like the Hummingbird, Woodpecker, Parrot, Pigeon, Sparrow, Duck, etc. God designed each type with the capacity for genetic variability as we see in dogs...allowing genetic variability within fixed limits. But dogs never turn into anything other than dogs; there are just different varieties of the same species. Every animal when it has offspring, has an offspring like it. Dogs don't have cats. All Noah had to have on the ark was *representatives* of each of the different *kinds* of animals, and there was plenty of room for these animal *representatives*. The Ark was an enormous boat...almost twice as long as a 747 Jumbo Jet, so *representatives* of all animals, including dinosaurs, had plenty of room to fit into it.

Noah's Ark was said to have been the largest sea-going vessel ever built until the late nineteenth century when giant metal ships were first constructed. The ship was so complex that it took Noah 120 years to build! Its length-to-width ratio of six-to-one provided excellent stability on the high seas... able to withstand 100ʹ waves! Modern shipbuilders say it would have been almost impossible to turn over. The total available floor space on the ark would have been over 100,000 square feet…more floor space than 20 standard-sized basketball courts. The total cubic volume would have been 1,518,000 cubic feet…equal to the capacity of 569 modern railroad stock cars!

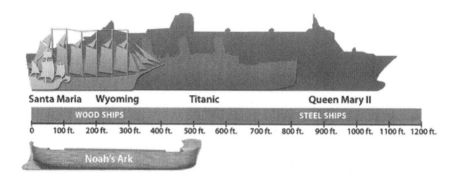

All Animals Did NOT Have to be Taken on the Ark!

God designed the Ark only to protect humans and land-dwelling, air-breathing creatures. My research found details of *a huge number of animals that did not need to be taken on board the Ark,* because they are water dwellers, quite capable of surviving the flood, thereby protecting them from extinction.

The Ark would not need to make any provision for the 21,000 species of fish, the 1,700 tunicates, the 600 echinoderms including starfish and sea urchins, or the 107,000 mollusks such as mussels, clams, and oysters, or the 10,000 coelenterates like corals and sea anemones, jelly fish, and hydroids, or the 5,000 species of sponges, or the 30,000 protozoans, the microscopic single-celled creatures.

In addition, some mammals are aquatic like whales, seals, and porpoises. Amphibians did not need to be included, nor reptiles, sea turtles, and alligators. A large number of arthropods (838,000 species) such as lobsters, shrimp, crabs, water fleas, and barnacles. And the insect species among arthropods are usually very small. The 35,000 species of worms as well as many insects could have survived outside the Ark.

A number of Biblical scholars state that no more than 35,000 and as few as 2,000 animals may have been required on the Ark, depending on the definition of the word, *specie,* and its equivalence to *created kinds* in the Genesis account. Most scholars agree that the Ark would accommodate at least 16,000 animals...but to satisfy skeptics, they expanded their estimate to 50,000 animals that could easily fit into the Ark.

There are really only a few very large animals, such as the dinosaur or the elephant, and these could be represented by young ones. Assuming the average animal to be about the size of a sheep and using a railroad car for comparison, the average double-deck stock car can accommodate 240 sheep. Therefore, three trains hauling 69 cars each would have ample space to carry 50,000 animals...still filling only 37% of the Ark's space. This would leave 361 cars or enough to make 5 trains of 72 cars each to carry all of the food and baggage plus Noah's family of eight people.

How the Animals Were Brought Into the Ark

There is a simple explanation for this as well. God never makes a plan without a solution. The Genesis account says that "*God (Himself) gathered the animals and brought them to Noah inside the Ark two by two.*" Problem solved! Others have suggested this incident could have been the origin of *migratory instinct…as* most animals possess the ability to sense danger and tend to move to safety.

Why Didn't the Carnivores Eat Up the Animal Inventory on the Ark?

A common *gotcha* question asked by the *nones and the doubters:* Wouldn't the carnivores have to eat up some of the *intended-to-be-preserved animal inventory of God's creation?* But if they closely examined the Biblical account and God's guidelines for his creations, they would learn that *there were no carnivores on the ark.* All living things were vegetarian until *after* the flood. After His initial creation—and <u>before</u> the flood—God said this, "*And to all the beasts of the earth and all the birds of the air and all the creatures that move on the ground—everything that has the breath of life in it—I give every* <u>green plant</u> *for food. And it was so.*" Genesis 1:30 But <u>after</u> the flood, God said this, "*Everything that lives and moves will be food for you. Just as I gave you the green plants, I now give you everything.*" Genesis 9:3

God Provided Noah with Animal Care-Taking Skills

Genesis 7:11-12 tell us that rain fell on the earth forty days and forty nights…flooding the earth 150 days. Imagine the problem Noah faced; he had only eight people to help him feed, water, provide fresh air and sanitation for the huge menagerie of animals for a total of 371 days. But since God created the animals, He certainly had the power to supernaturally have them go into a type of hibernation or dormancy, slowing down their bodily functions to a minimum. This would have reduced the burden of animal care for Noah and his family.

God's Design Enabled Plants to Survive the Flood

A final word about the destruction by the flood on the planet. Botanists tell us that many terrestrial seeds can survive for long periods of soaking in various concentrations of salt water. In fact, salt water actually impedes the germination of certain species so that the seed lasts better in salt water than in fresh water. During the flood, plants could have survived in floating vegetation masses and on pumice from volcanic activity. Pieces of many plants are also capable of *asexual sprouting.* Also many plants could have survived from foods stored on the Ark as food for Noah and his family as commanded by God in Genesis 6:21.

Many seeds are also designed with the ability to attach themselves to animals that came aboard the Ark and could have survived the flood in this manner. Other seeds could have survived in the stomachs of bloated, floating carcasses of dead herbivores. The olive leaf brought back to Noah by the dove (Genesis 8:11) was evidence that plants were already regenerating prior to Noah leaving the Ark.

Finding Noah's Ark

The photograph above is *visual evidence* of what is believed to be Noah's Ark. In 1959, Turkish army captain Lihan Durupiar discovered an unusual shape while examining aerial photographs of his country. The smooth shape, larger than a football field, stood out from the rough and rocky terrain at an altitude of 6,300 feet near the Turkish border of Iran. As the captain was familiar with the Bible account of the Ark and its association with Mt. Ararat in Turkey and since no previous reports of an object this odd had been made before, he forwarded the photographic negative to a famous aerial photography expert named Dr. Brandenburger at Ohio State University. Incidentally, Brandenburger was responsible for discovering the Cuban missile bases during the Kennedy administration. After examining the photographs, he concluded that he had no doubts that this object was a man-made ship—not a result of natural geology—quite probably Noah's Ark.

Once the physical site was examined and the measurements of the object surveyed, the findings reported the distance from bow to stern to be 300 Egyptian cubits, and the average width was 50 cubits. These measurements corresponded with the exact measurements mentioned in the Bible. Core samples taken from an open cavity on the starboard side revealed some objects which turned out to be petrified animal dung, a petrified antler, and a piece of cat hair.

In case you doubt these findings, another plausible explanation is that Noah and his family probably used the Ark to build houses for themselves and for fire wood. With everything buried under tons of mud from the flood, using the boat for more immediate and personal needs would be the logical thing to do. Most Christians accept that approximately 4400 years have lapsed since the flood, so expecting to find the Ark *intact* would be highly improbable due to natural deterioration.

Many Noted Scholars Date the Earth in 1000s of Years

According to the Bible, the earth is about 6000 years old, based upon the six days of creation. The genealogies in the Bible state the age of each man at the time he had his children. If one accepts the genealogies as literal history (as Christians do), then from Adam to Jesus is about 4000 years + another 2000 years from Jesus to present = 6000 years.

Other proofs that the earth is young include the fact that there are not enough people in the world; not enough salt in the ocean; the moon is moving further away every year; the oldest tree is too young; and the oldest coral reef is too young; and many geological engineers also agree that the geological systems of the earth have been made within 1000s of years—not millions or billions!

It matters that the earth is 1000s of years old and not millions, because there has not been enough time for the origin of life to have occurred *by chance*...as the evolutionists claim. Neither could the process of evolution develop all the creatures on the earth. Since the earth is young, life on earth was created by God.

The flood of Noah's day was a universal judgment of sin. God destroyed the world that existed at that time because of their wickedness. The flood is also a perfect picture of God's saving grace toward those who believe, trust, and follow His instructions for *eternal safety from the storms of sin.*

Finally, I heard Dr. Adrian Rogers say in a sermon, that Evolutionists and Athiests cannot answer these four questions: *1. What is the origin of life?* (How does life come from non-life?) *2. What about the fixity of the species?* (Why do we have mutation, but never transmutation?) *3. What about the Second Law of Thermodynamics—everything is subject to death, decay, and disintegration?* (Can time plus chance turn frogs into princes?) *4. Where did non-physical properties originate*—music, art, and a hunger for God?

A Few of God's Animal Wows

Zebras – The stripes of Zebras make them one of the most familiar animals. It was originally believed that they were white with black stripes, but embryological evidence proved the contrary—the animal's background is black with white stripes and white underbellies. A variety of hypotheses have been proposed to explain the stripes of Zebras, but the consensus relate to camouflage. It is believed that the striping helps them hide in grass, and at even moderate distances the striping seen by predators either merges into an apparent grey color or may confuse predators by *motion dazzle*...making it difficult for the lion to select a *kill* target. Research also found that the Zebra's striping is minimally attractive to horseflies. It seems that horseflies are attracted to linearly-polarized light, and the black and white striping disrupts this pattern. Most interesting is that God designed a striping pattern that is *unique to each individual Zebra.* The mother is able to recognize the unique striping of her newborn from a herd, and it also serves as identification cues to other Zebras.

Salamanders – More species of the salamander are found in The Americas than in the entire rest of the world combined. There are 500 species of Salamanders,  and they come in a variety of color patterns. God also gave *each* of the spotted Salamanders a *unique pattern of spots.*

Salamanders are capable of regenerating lost limbs as well as other body parts including tails and toes within a few weeks, allowing them to survive attacks from predators. Some species are poisonous; some have teeth; and some have tongues 10 times longer than their bodies. The Giant Chinese Salamander—the largest species in the world—can weigh up to 140 pounds, grow to a length of 10 feet, and they have a life span of 55-75 years.

Camels – There are two types of Camels: the Dromedary one-hump camel of the hot deserts of North Africa and south western Asia; and the two-hump Bactrian camel, native to the Gobi Desert in Mongolia. The Dromedary can go with- 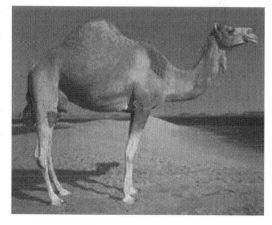 out food and water 8 days. Their thick coats reflect sunlight and serve to insulate them from the heat of the sand and sun. They live about 50 years and can run up to 40 mph. Camels can close their nostrils to prevent sand from entering inside their nose.

Camels are herbivores eating mainly dry leaves, seeds, and desert plants. Camels are ruminants, meaning they can regurgitate previously swallowed but undigested food and re-chew it. When food is scarce, the camel automatically uses fat from the hump as an emergency food supply. When the hump is used up, it falls limp to the side, but as soon as he begins to eat, the hump plumps up again.

The camel has been known to drink 27 gallons of water in 10 minutes. Scientists studies show that after 10 minutes of drinking 20 gallons of water, camels can carry a 400 pound load 100 miles across a hot, dry desert and not stop once for a drink. After 10 minutes of drinking, the camel can gain back 227 pounds lost!

Normally, the blood of a camel contains 94% water, just like man, but when they can't find water, the heat of the sun gradually robs a little water from his blood. Scientists have found that blood of camels can lose up to 40% of it its water and still be healthy. Doctors say human blood must stay very close to the 94% level. If man loses only 5% of his blood's water content, he can't see anymore; lose 10%, he can't hear and goes insane; lose 12%, and man's blood becomes thick like molasses, and his heart can't pump it, and he dies! Man's blood cells are round. The camel's blood cells are elongated. God designed these differences…for a purpose. The camel is designed for the desert. A good question for the agnostic is, *did you ever hear of a design without a Designer?*

The Intelligent Designer also gave the camel a specially-designed nose that preserves water. When the camel exhales, his nose traps the warm, moist air from his lungs. Tiny blood vessels in those membranes recycle that warm moisture back into his blood. The camel's nose is 18 degrees cooler than the rest of his body. The camel has special muscles in his nostrils that close the nose openings, keeping sand out of his nose, but allowing enough air to breathe.

Even the camel's eyelashes are specially designed to arch down over his eyes like screens...keeping the sun out but still allowing him to see clearly. If a grain of sand gets into the camel's eye, the Master Designer took care of that too. The camel has an *inner eyelid* that acts as a windshield wiper, wiping the sand off the eye!

The camel was designed not only to provide unique transportation for people living in the desert areas, but also to provide very rich milk that can be made into butter and cheese. Young camels are also a beef substitute. And even his thick coat of fur is shed once a year that inhabitants of the region weave into cloth.

The creative majesty of this world is a mystery that will continue to unfold until we get to eternity. All of the above facts are just a few examples that these animals were *highly engineered* by the *Master Designer*. God's infinite intelligence and creativity are declared in all His designs—the Heavens, the earth, and everything in it *"so that we are without excuse."* (Romans 1:20) Any attempt by man's *"wisdom"* to be dismissive or try to explain away God as the Intelligent Designer, God sees as *"foolishness."* (1 Corinthians 3:19)

"Similarly there are different kinds of flesh—one kind for humans, another for animals, another for birds, and another for fish." 1 Corinthians 15:39

Chapter Twelve

Day Six: (Part B.) Man, God's Masterpiece

"From one man he made all the nations, that they should inhabit the whole earth; and he marked out their appointed times in history and the boundaries of their lands." Acts 17:26

Race

According to the Bible, there is only one race—the human race. All humans on earth today are descendants from Noah and his wife, his three sons and their wives...even though today it seems that we have many different races with different features such as skin color, eye shape, and language. Prior to the flood, all descendants were from Adam and Eve.

But the Bible tells us that following the flood, all people spoke one language, living in one place, in disobedience to God's command to *"fill the earth."* (Genesis 9:1, 11:4) So God confused their language, breaking up the population into smaller groups which scattered over the earth. (Genesis 11:8-9) Modern study of genetics now show that following the break-up of a population, variations in skin color can develop in just a few generations for these people groups...not 1000s of years as evolutionists say. All civilized cultures on earth seem to have appeared *suddenly* approximately 5000 years ago.

Anthropologists classify people into a small number of main *racial groups:* Caucasoid (European or White), the Mongoloid (Chinese, Inuit or Eskimo, and Native Americans), the Negroid (black Africans), and the Australoid (the Australian Aborigines). Even evolutionists now agree that the various people groups <u>*did not*</u> *have separate origins*—evolving from a different group of animals.

All peoples can interbreed and produce fertile offspring. This is proof that the biological differences between *races* or *people groups* are not great. In fact, the DNA differences are trivial…differing between any two people in the world by just 0.2%. Of this 0.2%, only 6% can be linked to racial categories…the rest is within race variations.

We all have the same coloring pigment in our skin, called melanin. This is a dark-brownish pigment that is produced in different amounts in special cells in our skin. If we had no melanin (as Albinos), we would have white or pink skin coloring. On the other hand, if our skin produced a lot of melanin, we would be very black. Other than melanin, there are no other significant skin pigments. We are not born with a genetically fixed amount of melanin, but rather a genetically fixed potential to produce a certain amount which increases in response to sunlight exposure. So we know that skin color is not evidence of a difference in the human genetic code.

We also know that different skin colors can result in a short time when we remember that different skin color refers to *different shades of the one color,* melanin. If a member of a very black people group marries someone from a very white people group, their offspring (called mulattos) are mid-brown in color. It's been known for a long time that when mulattos marry each other, their offspring may range from very dark to very light.

Whatever feature we may look at, no people group has anything that is essentially different from that possessed by another. For example, the Asian or *almond eye* differs from a typical Caucasian eye in having more fat around them. Both Asian and Caucasian eyes have fat—the latter simply have less.

Language

"The heavens declare the glory of God; the skies proclaim the work of his hand. Day after day they pour forth speech; night after night they display knowledge. There is no speech or language where their voice is not heard. Their voice goes out into all the earth, their words to the end of the world." Psalm 19:14

It is a fact that most ancient cultures began in an advanced state. There is no trace of *"primitive"* generations leading up to the sudden explosion of *"advanced"* civilizations across the world. The sudden appearance of rational, creative, and very intelligent beings supports what the Bible states...*that man was made in God's image.* (Genesis 1:27) The intricacy and stability of the great pyramids in Egypt are examples of re-markable human engineering...*by an ancient people.*

Genesis opens with the Creator creating an intelligible world with intelligent beings endowed with the tool of language which enabled them to comprehend, communicate, and use information. Linguists agree that language presupposes relationships—correlations between objects and subjects, causes and effects, sensory inputs and human perceptions, man and his environment, matter and energy, forces and the objects they effect.

Yes, *prototype man* was created and *factory-equipped* with language built in. Evidence of this is that as soon as God formed Adam from the dust of the earth, He spoke with Adam and Eve and gave them instructions they *understood—multiply, name the flora, and fauna, etc.* And we know that Eve had *conversations* with Satan in the Garden of Eden about partaking of the forbidden fruit. All this was evidence that God spoke with man and that man understood language.

The Human Body…Extraordinary Design

The human body is a treasure trove of mysteries, and it's not an overstatement to say that every part of our bodies is a miracle. For example, without the stomach, the spleen, 75% of the liver, 80% of the intestines, one kidney, one lung, and virtually every organ in the pelvic and groin area, the body is able to survive! Let's start with a selection of random facts about the human body that I found in a quick search on the internet…

- Your body is made up of 100 trillion cells…considerably more than America's current national debt!

- Each second, 10,000,000 cells die and are replaced in your body.

- You have 22 internal organs, 600 muscles, and 206 bones.

- Your liver performs over 500 functions in your body.

- *You* started from an egg 0.2mm in diameter.

- The egg—produced inside your mother when she herself was an embryo—is the *largest* cell in the human body; male sperm the *smallest*.

- Your tongue, finger, voice, and eye prints are all unique.

- Your skin is the largest organ of your body, shedding about 1.5 pounds of skin each year...by age 70, average skin shedding = 105 lbs.

- Approximately 32 million bacteria cover every inch of your skin most of which are harmless...some even beneficial.

- Babies start with 350 bones, but after fusing together, as adults have only 206 bones.

- A solid piece of bone the size of a matchbox can support the weight of 9 tons...more weight than a block of concrete can support.

- The digestive juices inside your stomach can dissolve zinc; fortunately, the stomach lining is renewed every 3-4 days or it would digest itself.

- Your body produces an average of 25,000 quarts of saliva over your lifetime.

- Your lungs have 700,000,000 cells of honeycomb, equal to a flat surface of 2000 square feet and inhale / exhale 11,000 liters of air daily.

- Your body has 1000 miles of blood vessels, yet it takes only 60 seconds for a human blood cell to make a complete circuit.

- 1/15th of a pint of blood is pumped with every heartbeat.

- Your nasal memory comprises 50,000 different scents.

- On average, your eyes blink 20,000 times a day.

- The focus muscles of your eyes move 100,000 times a day; compared to walking, that's a distance of 50 miles.

- One human brain cell can hold 5 times the information of an encyclopedia.

- Nerve impulses travel to and from the brain as fast as 170 mph.

- Your brain does not feel pain, is 75% water, uses 20% of your body's energy, and yet represents only 2% of your body's weight.

- Your sneeze can exceed speeds over 100 mph.

- It takes the interaction of 72 different muscles to produce human speech.

- If the average 250,000 hairs on your head were woven into a rope, it could support a weight of more than 12 tons.

- Your heart beats 100,000 times a day, averaging over 2 ½ billion times by age 70—without a break for over a lifetime!

- You inhale about 7 quarts of air every minute.

DNA...Divine Design of Man's Blueprint

It's been said that it's now becoming blaringly apparent that *"the ship of evolution has run aground."* The Darwinian *Theory* is being rejected by a rapidly-growing number of prominent microbiologists after studying the complexities of the human cell using scanning tunneling microscopy (STM). And recent scientific discoveries within the human cell continue to reveal incredible entities that defy evolutionary explanation.

Just as a blueprint describes a building, our DNA carries information in our bodies that determines we will be human, rather than a cantaloupe or crocodile. It also specifies each detail of how each person will be built...our eye and hair color, our height, facial features. The human blueprint is written in a code or language on very long chemical strings of our DNA. DNA is by far the most efficient

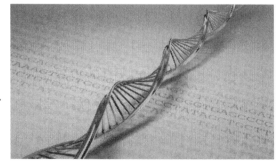

information storage system known...greatly surpassing even any *foreseeable* computer technology. Boggling the mind is the fact that this information is *efficiently* copied and reshuffled again and again—*without compromise*—from generation to generation as people reproduce.

Then there's the *gene* which refers to a small part of this DNA information string that carries the instructions for only *one type of enzyme.* Think of it as a portion of the *DNA message string* containing only one specification, like the instructions for making hemoglobin—the protein that carries oxygen in your red blood cells. If there are *copying mistakes* during reproduction, the result could be sickle-cell anemia. But the good news is that *genes come in pairs*—one from the father and one from the mother. So if one parent's gene is damaged, bad results could be offset by the good gene from the other parent...our Creator's *original back-up system!*

Chapter Thirteen

The Cell: God's Signature

I *skimmed* through all 509 pages of Stephen C. Meyer's book, *Signature in the Cell: DNA and the Evidence for Intelligent Design* (ID) *before* attempting to *simplify and condense* this significantly important section 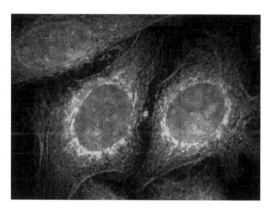 on the cell. I say, *skimmed,* because even though I too have a Ph.D., I am mentally dwarfed and humbled by the intricacies of Meyer's brilliant, scientific mind, as he presents *scientific* evidence of *God's "signature in the cell."* His research notes, bibliography, and index *alone* took up almost 100 *additional* pages to the 509 pages...that I *skimmed.*

In this scholarly and exciting read, Meyer contends that Intelligent Design is the best explanation for the origin of life, citing *pro-con* evidence from both *front-load* proponents (Darwinians) and also the ID contenders. Meyer makes the case that no physical or chemical entity or process could *independently* produce the complex amounts of information necessary to produce the first life, roughly 500 bits or more. As a layman, my take is that, God *copy-protected ALL life-design information and instructions for each cell's designated purpose by incorporating it into each CELL'S DNA.* In just one human cell there is 6.5 feet of DNA. In the whole human body, there are 10-20 *billion* miles of DNA throughout one *trillion* cells! There are up to a *trillion to 1000 trillion* DNA in a typical human cell!

Physicist, John Archibald Wheeler, put it this way, "Every physical quantity derives its ultimate significance from bits, binary yes-or-no indications." In *computer-ese*, that's *information.* He says that the fundamental ingredient of the material world in fact is *not material, but rather information,* and the existence of information is evidence that reality is more than matter. Even more important is the fact that God is not only the *Author* of all information but also the *Designer* of man's brain and subsequent ability to acquire, understand, process, and utilize information!

Anthropologists who discovered the ancient cave paintings in Lascaux, France, recognized that the only cause capable of producing this *representational* art was the presence of *intelligent* beings. Meyer began to wonder if there might be a similarly-based argument for concluding that *Intelligent Design (ID)* played a role in the origin of *biological information.* I've summarized his reasoning below...

1. *There is no other causally-adequate explanation.* In his examination of *chance, necessity, and the combination of the two,* he found these theories did not reveal any cause or process capable of generating biologically-relevant amounts of specified information other than *ID.*

2. *Experimental Evidence Confirms Causal Adequacy of ID.* Since intelligent human beings by virtue of their rationality and consciousness have the power to produce specified information, why not explore whether there is evidence in support of the *causal* power of *Intelligent Design*—the *necessity of* a mind to arrange matter into structures relevant to life."

3. *ID Is the Only Known Cause of Specified Information.* After exploring *ALL* origin-of-life theories Meyer determined that "*undirected* materialistic causes have *not* demonstrated the capacity to generate significant amounts of specified information." By contrast, conscious *intelligence* repeatedly shows the capability of producing such information. It follows that an intelligent designer (God) stands as the *only* cause known that is capable of generating large amounts of specified information...*starting from a non-living state.*

Let's look a little more closely at the cells of our body, these *very tiny efficient machines* that Meyer calls, "God's Signature." During the course of a normal life span, every cell in the body, including the brain, is replaced many times over. The molecules that make up our bodies are constantly undergoing many changes; *yet those changes have no significant effect on the instructions that govern cell activity.*

The many miniature machines and circuits that have been discovered in cells by chemists and molecular biologists—such as the bacterial flagella motor—provide some of the strongest evidence for *Intelligent Design*. The interactions of the many parts of these cell machines could not have developed from an undirected random mutation (or evolutionary) process. There could not have been an original *super cell* from which all others *"mutated"* because *"Darwin's natural selection"* can only act on what mutations *first* generate. Different types of cells contain *specific design proteins*, and these *design-specific* proteins would have to be in the *"original cell."*

Proteins Conduct *Nano-Scale* Electricity

A team from the Cardiff University's Schools of Biosciences, Physics, and Astronomy made a significant breakthrough in understanding proteins—the workhorse molecules of the cell and nature's very own *nano machines*. A team of molecular biologists found that at the single-molecule level a protein can conduct a large amount of electricity. They also discovered that *current flow* could be regulated in much the same way as transistors—those tiny devices driving computers and smartphones—but just on a smaller scale. These proteins are only a quarter of the size of current silicon-based transistors. Prior to this team's work, the existing protein research had to be done on millions, even billions of proteins. But this team, using scanning tunneling microscopy (STM), was able to read the electronics of a single molecule of cytochrome b562…a protein just 5 nanometers (billions of a meter) long!

From all my research, I found that Michael Denton provided the most vivid description of the cell in his book,

"Evolution: A Theory in Crisis." He takes us on a *virtual tour* <u>inside</u> the cell…

"To grasp the reality of life as it has been revealed by molecular biology, we must magnify a cell *a thousand million times* (italics mine) until it is 20 kilometers in diameter and resembles a giant airship large enough to cover a great city like London or New York. What we would then see would be an object of unparalleled complexity and adaptive design. On the surface of the cell we would see millions of openings like the portholes of a vast spaceship, opening and closing to allow a continual stream of materials to flow in and out. If we were to enter one of the openings we would find ourselves in a world of supreme technology and bewildering complexity. We would see endless highly organized corridors and conduits branching in every direction away from the perimeter of the cell, some leading to the central memory bank in the nucleus and others to the assembly plants and processing units. The nucleus itself would be a vast spherical chamber more than a kilometer in diameter, resembling a geodesic cone inside of which we would see all neatly stacked together in ordered arrays, the miles of coiled chains of DNA molecules."

Here is the best analogy I found that describes the incredible amount of information stored in human DNA: "It would fill *12 sets of the Encyclopedia Britannica—34 volumes—which would fill 48 feet of library shelves. The length of DNA present in one human being is 200 times the distance from earth to the sun!"*

In his book, *"Darwin's Black Box,"* Michael Behe also writes of some single-cell organisms found within the human body, like sperm cells and certain bacterial flagella which have long, whip-like tails enabling them to swim in fluids. Behe reports these flagella are powered by a molecular motor similar to an outboard motor. *Each motor has a rotor, a stator, a driveshaft, bearings, u-joint, and propeller!* Does this sound like *chance* to you?

If one is seriously looking for evidence of *Intelligent Design,* one needs to look no further than the incredible design-complexity of the human cell. And where there is *design,* there must be a *Designer.*

"For thou didst form my inward parts; Thou didst weave me in my mother's womb. I will give thanks to Thee, for I am fearfully and wonderfully made; wonderful are Thy works, and my soul knows it very well. My frame was not hidden from Thee, when I was made in secret, and skillfully wrought in the depths of the earth." Psalm 139:13-15

Chapter Fourteen

The Sum of Many Parts

"But our bodies have many parts, and God has put each part just where He wants it." "In fact, some parts of the body that seem weakest and least important are actually the most necessary." 1 Corinthians 12:18; 1 Corinthians 12:22

Bones – Let's begin by taking a look at the bones that our Creator Architect designed—*the lightest structure, made of the least material, to support the weight of our bodies.* This is a weight-saving architectural principal that took 1000s of years for man to discover. Our bones have been described as *quiet and dependable, getting our attention only when we encounter fractures beyond their high tolerance.* Take the foot for example. The 26 bones in each foot, along with a perfectly-designed arch, bending knees, and ankles, will take us 2 ½ times around the world in a lifetime. *One-fourth of the bones in the human body are in the feet!*

The 27 bones in our hands are marvels of maneuverability with 70 separate muscles contributing to hand movement, although there are no muscles in the actual fingers. Despite years of research and multi-millions of dollars spent, scientist-designed, *atomic-age hands are like Play Doh sculpture compared to a Michelangelo masterpiece!* Atomic-age hands are pathetically clumsy juxtaposed to the dexterity of God's design of the human hand that allows us to grasp, retain, and handle objects easily and precisely.

All bones in our bodies are arranged in perfectly-engineered, intersecting lines of stress, like the girders on a steel bridge. Our Creator Architect took this stress-bearing bone, hollowed it out, and filled in the vacant space with an efficient red-blood cell factory that produces *a trillion new cells a day!*

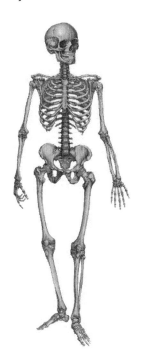

When we look at a human skeleton, we probably focus on functionality and strength rather than its beauty. The most important feature of bone and the one property that separates it from other tissue in the body is its hardness. But when one is confined to bed for prolonged periods, the bones will lose up to 50% of the calcium. Astronauts lose up to 20% of their bone mass due to lack of gravity in space.

The human skeleton is the internal framework of our body. We begin with up to 350 bones at birth, but this total decreases to 206 bones by adulthood after some bones have fused together. When we're young, 100% of all the bone in our bodies is replaced every year, but thanks to our Creator's design of our DNA, the shape of our new bones stay the same, only larger. As adults, only about 18% gets replaced each year. If a surgeon cuts into one of our bones, it bleeds, but most amazing of all, the *bone begins to heal itself!*

So, here's a question for the *"nones"* – What engineer could design a substance like bone that is *light weight, incredibly strong, grows continuously, lubricates itself, requires no shut-down time, and even repairs itself when damage occurs?*

<u>*The Backbone*</u> - Think back to your early days in high-school biology class where you learned there were two categories of animals—vertebrates (those with a backbone or spine) and invertebrates (those without). God designed approximately 4% of all the animals on earth with backbones; the rest are invertebrates. Without our spines, we would literally fall to the ground in a heap!

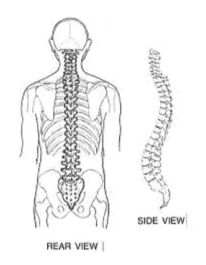

SIDE VIEW

REAR VIEW

Running down the middle of our backs is a bony center column that not only allows us to walk about in an upright position, but also provides a protective covering for the *critical bundle of nerves* connecting to the brain. These nerves carry feeling and send split-second signals to our muscles that make us walk and accomplish every human activity.

Envision God's brilliant design of the spine as 24 donuts with a hole in the middle, stacked on top of each other to form a tunnel that protects these critical nerves inside the spinal column. This tunnel of 24 vertebrae *articulate* or move because there are flat, gelatinous pads or *discs* that cushion the *moveable* vertebrae. When the discs *slip* or *deteriorate,* excruciating pain results. By the time we reach adulthood, there are an additional 9 *fused vertebrae* located at the bottom of the spinal column forming the sacrum and coccyx.

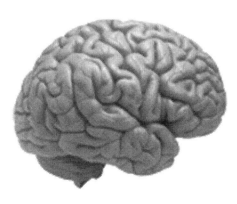

The Brain – The human brain—often referred to as *the seat of the soul*—was the pinnacle of God's creation. His plan was that man would use it for the purpose of getting to know Him. We should never take our brains for granted, because even more than our hearts, our brains are staggeringly-amazing organs that are critical to our survival. Without our brains to process information, we would never know what we are feeling, seeing, hearing, smelling, tasting, or touching. We would never dream, be able to reason, record, or remember anything that has ever happened to us. Man would be without an interest in or an appetite for exploring, questioning, gathering knowledge...incapable of inventing, or building cities. Senses such as care, empathy, pride, patriotism, shame, love, and forgiveness would be unknowns.

Here are just a few interesting facts about this amazing God-designed *biological computer...*

- The brain is a squishy, pinkish, jelly-like organ made up of 100,000 miles of blood vessels; it is 80% water and 60% fat.

- The *cerebrum* represents about 85% of the brain's total weight of approximately 3 lbs.

- The estimated storage capacity of the brain is between 3 and 1000 *terabytes!* (FYI: A terabyte is a little over 1000 gigabytes!) By comparison, Britain's National Archives stores 900 years of information for their entire country in only 70 terabytes.

- The human brain receives and processes millions of simultaneous reports from the eye cells.

- The brain's *grey matter* is made up of about *100 billion neurons* that gather and transmit signals.

- There are between *1000 and 10,000 synapses PER NEURON!*

- The brain's *white matter* is made up of *dendrites and axons*—the *network of transmitters* used by the neurons to transmit signals.

- Every time we recall a memory or have a new thought, the brain creates a *new connection.*

- While awake, the brain generates 10-23 watts of *electrical power* for processing information.

- Neurons in the brain process information at different speeds, depending on the type of information, but messages can travel faster than racecars—*up to 268 mph.*

- The brain uses 20% of our circulating blood and 20% of the oxygen we breathe, yet represents only 2% of our body mass.

- The brain never sleeps; in fact, it's even more active at night while we sleep.

- Since neurons can and do regenerate, the brain can *"heal"* itself to some extent, depending on the damage.

- There are no pain receptors in the brain, so the brain itself feels no pain.

- Humans have the largest brains proportionate to body size.

- Music lessons, juggling, and learning another language have been shown to boost brain organization and ability.

- It's been estimated that humans have over 70,000 thoughts a day.

- Touching something sends a message to your brain *at 124 mph!*

The Five Senses

"The human body has many parts...and if the ear says, I am not a part of the body because I am not an eye...if the whole body were an eye, how would you hear...or if your whole body

were an ear, how would you smell anything?" (Portions selected from 1 Corinthians 12:12-17)

The five senses—sight, hearing, taste, touch, and smell—
enable us to *make sense* of the world around us, and scientists
are still discovering new things about these marvelous mira-
cles.Let's start with sight...

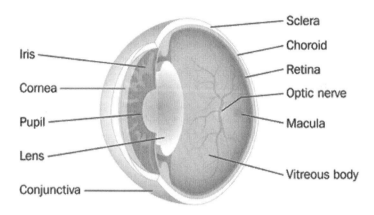

<u>Sight</u> – God created man *in the beginning,* endowing him
with two magnificent eyes. The eye has often been compared
with the camera, yet it wasn't until 1840 that man invented
the first camera to record what man sees.

Simply stated, eyes detect light and allow us to see. Although
we think we *see with our eyes,* what we really see are interpreta-
tions or *translations* by the brain. In fact, 50% of the brain remains involved in the seeing process. The human brain's *visual
cortex* is more developed than that of any other mammal.

In the retina alone, there are about 6 million light-sensitive
cone cells and another 100 million or so light-sensitive rods.

Looking then at the optic nerve, the cornea, and the lens, there are many million more specialized cells.

The eye is designed to differentiate between foreground and background, separate edges from lines, make sense of shapes and symbols, and organize fragments of light and darkness into coherent wholes. Magicians and artists have fun creating *optical illusions* by exploiting the brain's tendency to find order in *impossible* patterns.

Everything we see is received by the retina upside-down, and since we have two eyes, we also have two retinas. So contrary to what you might think, we do not see two of everything. The reason we don't see two distinct images is the same reason we don't see everything upside-down. The brain is constantly processing this visual information, combining the two images into one, and *turning the images right-side-up*. Here are a few interesting quick facts about the *eye and sight…*

- The human eye can detect 10 million color hues, but cannot see ultraviolet or infra-red light; only insects can!

- Eyes blink 12 times per minute, about 10,000 blinks a day, using our tears to clean the eyeball.

- Eyes can process 36,000 bits of information every hour.

- The human eye has 6 external muscles to control its movement and are the strongest muscles in the body for the job they do!

- This phenomenal tool for gathering light can distinguish 500 shades of gray and see the lumen of one candle up to 14 miles away!

- The eye can focus on about 50 things per second.

- Eyelashes protect our eyes by keeping dirt out.

- The eye's *cornea* is the only living tissue in the human body that does not contain any blood vessels!

- It's impossible to sneeze with your eyes open.

The prophet, Isaiah, delivered God's judgment upon the people who refused to believe and continued to follow after false gods in spite of the miracles that God performed. They would lose their ability to *see, hear, and believe...*

> *"Go and tell this people, Hear ye indeed, but understand not; and see ye indeed, but perceive not. Make the heart of this people fat, and make their ears heavy, and shut their eyes; lest they see with their eyes, and hear with their ears, and understand with their heart."*
> Isaiah 6:9

<u>Hearing</u> – The two ears are our organs for hearing and balance. Here's the short explanation of the God-designed *miracle* of hearing. When sound waves hit our eardrums, the eardrum vibrates, and the brain interprets these vibrations as sound. But in order to better understand this miraculous

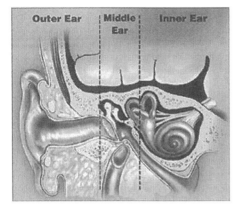

sense of hearing, we need a few more details.

The ear consists of three sections—the *outer ear*, the *middle ear*, and *inner ear*. The *outer ear*—the part that can be seen on each side of the head—directs the sound into the *ear canal* on the way to the *eardrum*. Near the *canal* entrance there are hairs and glands that produce wax to keep our ears clean. When sound from the outside reaches the *eardrum* at the end of the *canal* it vibrates. After these sound vibrations hit our *eardrums,* a chain reaction is set off.

The *eardrum* (which is smaller and thinner than the nail on our pinky finger) sends these vibrations to the *middle-ear bones*—the three smallest bones in our bodies—the *malleus,* the *incus,* and the *stapes.* After sound enters our ears, making the *eardrum* vibrate, the vibrations pass from the *eardrum* through the *middle-ear bones.* The last bone to receive the vibration, the *stapes,* then pushes like a piston against the membrane entrance to the *inner ear.*

The *inner ear* has two parts, both of which are encased in bone—the *cochlea,* used for hearing; and the *vestibular,* used for balance. The *cochlea* is a spiral tube that is coiled like a snail shell. This spiral tube contains two fluid-filled chambers—an *outer* and *inner* chamber. The *stapes* pushes the vibrations into the fluid in the outer chamber. The *inner* chamber of the cochlea contains the organ of *Corti* which has about 17,000 small hair *cells* along the length of the *cochlea*. Each *cell* has tiny hair-like structures called *stereocilia* which project into the *cochlear fluid*. These *hair cells* connect to the *auditory nerve* which goes from the *cochlea* to the *brain*.

Also located in the top of the *cochlea* are three loops called the *semi-circular canal*. The canals are full of fluid that moves when our heads move, sending messages to the brain telling us how our bodies are moving.

Here are some other interesting facts about *sound and the miracle of hearing*...

- Doctors tell us that babies with pristine hearing have the ability to distinguish between 300,000 sounds.

- Our brains process sound 1000 times faster than sight, even registering sounds while we sleep, but the brain *turns off the sound*. This hypersensitivity to sound is God's gift of *early-warning* protection from danger.

- For young children it's been estimated that 90% of learning is associated with the ability to hear the background conversations within their environment.

- Although our ears enable us to determine the direction of sound, our ears are less accurate at assessing the distance of the sound.

- Eardrums can pick up sounds so faint that the eardrum moves a distance *less than the diameter of a hydrogen molecule!*

- Studies warn that continuous exposure to loud noises contributes significantly to hearing loss, and that living in loud areas can raise blood pressure an average of 5 to 8%. Even small noises cause the pupils of the eyes to dilate.

- Dolphins' hearing is 14 times better than that of humans.

- The smallest bones in the human body—the *malleus, incus, and stapes*—could fit on top of a penny.

- The whole area of the *middle ear* is the size of an M & M.

- The *cochlea* or *inner ear* is about the size of a pencil eraser.

- Sound travels at the speed of 1130 feet per second (770 mph).

- A baby's cry logs in at 115 dB…louder than a car horn.

- Because of their quiet environment, an African tribe (Maabans) can hear a whisper from the distance of a baseball field away.

- At birth, the human ear can hear sounds as *low* as 20 Hertz (lower than the lowest note on a piano) and as *high* as 20,000 Hertz (higher than the highest note on a piccolo.)

- Sitting in front of speakers at a rock concert can expose a person to 120 dB, which will begin to damage your hearing in only 7 ½ minutes.

"How can they call on the one they have not believed in? And how can they believe in the one of whom they have not heard? And how can they hear without someone preaching to them?" Romans 10:14

<u>Taste</u> – Did you ever stop to thank God for His gracious gift of taste? He designed taste so we could enjoy the flavors of all the foods he made. We experience the taste of something by way of the 10,000 taste buds on the tongue. These taste buds (papillae) are the tiny bumps you can see on your tongue. Each taste bud is the home to gustatory cells in charge of the tasting chore. Interwoven among these cells is a network of taste nerves. Food particles flow into the taste bud, and these taste-nerve cells send signals to the "taste center" of the brain's cortex. There, the brain discerns whether a food tastes good or bad. Once these taste signals reach the brain other neural pathways are stimulated

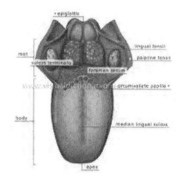

that contribute to the digestive process, like increased salivation and changes in activities in the stomach.

The sense of smell also plays a significant part in the sense of taste. In the upper part of your nose there are special cells that help you smell during the chewing process. Nasal congestion disrupts our sense of taste and diminishes the sense of taste due to the cold.

In addition to the tongue, taste buds are also located on the roof of the mouth (palate) and on the throat, working together to give sensations of sweet, sour, bitter, salty, and metallic tastes. Taste preferences change over time, and as we age some taste buds are not replaced. Older adults may have only half the number of taste buds of a younger person. Studies show that changes in food preferences appear in conjunction with what our bodies need. Interestingly, these changes in food and taste preferences originate in the central nervous system rather than directly through our taste cells, although scientists are at a loss why this is true.

Here are some other interesting quick facts about *taste...*

- It is believed that the design of *taste* had 2 purposes— defense against poison; and pleasure.

- *Taste* detection is *lightning fast,* as little as .0015 seconds (compared with .0024 for *touch,* .013 for *vision.*

- Most humans are born with a *sweet tooth.*

- Studies show that babies prefer foods they first *tasted* in the womb or while nursing; garlic and vanilla traces have shown up in amniotic fluid and breast milk.

- About 25% of Americans have been identified as *super-tasters* (have more taste buds and elevated sensitivity to bitter foods); also an equal number of *non-tasters* (fewer taste buds) who have a higher tolerance for spicy foods.

- Our taste buds die off and regenerate every few days; but regeneration cycle slows with age.

- Food scientists are experimenting with additives that trick our taste buds into perceiving sweetness without sugar.

"O taste and see that the Lord is good: blessed is the man that trusts in him." Psalm 34:8

<u>Touch</u> – Of all our senses, some believe touch is the most difficult to imagine doing without. The skin is the body's largest organ, and there are 100s of nerve endings in every square inch of skin. These nerve endings serve as antennae for receiving a steady stream of information from everything that touches the body within its environment. Touch is the first sense we develop in utereo, and God designed it as crucial to survival. Babies can die for lack of it, and as adults, touch helps to protect us from harm. Our nerves in our skin are quite specialized—some feel pressure; some detect temperature or register pain; and some sense the position of our bodies in space. Here are some other interesting facts about *touch*...

- The skin contains more than 4 million sensory receptors.

- The most sensitive areas on the body are the lips, back of the neck, the fingertips, and soles of the feet.

- The least sensitive area of the body is the middle of the back.

- Touch reduces stress by lowering the levels of hormones.

- The skin has more receptors for pain than for any other sensation.

- Thermo-receptors perceive sensations related to temperature, but do not function when the surface of the skin falls below 41 degrees, resulting in numbness.

- When the temperature of the skin rises above 113 degrees, the receptors for pain take over.

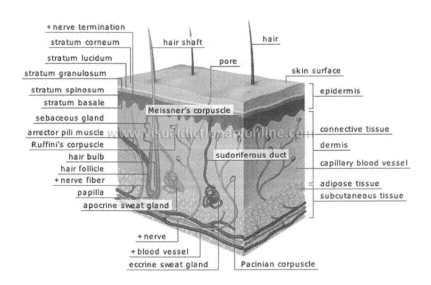

"Moved with compassion, Jesus touched their eyes; and immediately they regained their sight." Matthew 20:34

<u>Smell</u> – The nose is our personal air-conditioning system; it warms cold air, cools hot air, and filters impurities. Smell may be our most memorable

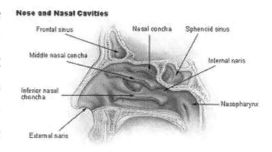

sense, as studies show that we can remember a scent with 65% accuracy after one year! Visual memory comes in at just 50% after just a few months. The temporal lobe—the part of the brain that processes memories and emotions—also handles smell. It's commonly reported that a passing scent can cue memories from years past. Although the human nose is not on par with our canine friends, we can detect the scent of a skunk when there is *one ten-trillionth of an ounce* in the air. The human nose is able to tell the direction from which the scent comes. Our sense of smell is quite individual, for example, some people cannot smell mushrooms or camphor. These differences are mostly genetic, but also can be temporarily affected by moods and certain medications which can both enhance and diminish our sense of smell.

According to new research by lead researcher, Dr. Andreas Keller of Rockefeller University and published in the journal Science, *the human nose can detect more than 1 trillion different smells,* suggesting we are much better at telling odors apart than the previously-thought 10,000 smells. (Definitely a God-Wow design!) It is thought that there are hundreds of different olfactory receptors, each encoded by a different gene and each recognizing different odors. Each of the hundreds of receptors are encoded by a specific gene. If your DNA is missing a gene or if the gene is damaged, it can cause you to be unable to detect a certain smell.

In order for you to smell something, molecules from that *thing* have to make it to your nose. Everything you smell, therefore, is molecules from the source—whether it is bread in the bakery, onions, perfume, a piece of fruit, or whatever. Those molecules are generally light or volatile (easy to evaporate) chemicals that float through the air into your nose. A piece of steel has no smell because nothing evaporates from it, as steel is a *non-volatile* solid.

At the top of your nasal passages behind your nose, there is a patch of special neurons about the size of a postage stamp. These neurons are unique in that they are out in the open where they can come into contact with the air. They have hair-like projections called cilia that increase their surface area. An odor molecule binds to these cilia to trigger the neuron and cause you to perceive a smell. When you smell many fruits or flowers, what you are smelling is *esters* (organic molecules) evaporating from the fruit or flower. What a generous and thoughtful gift from God the sense of smell is!

<u>The Heart</u> – We are told in Genesis 2:7 that *"God formed man from the dust of the ground and breathed into his nostrils the breath of life, and the man became a living soul."*

The Heart is the organ that causes us to *live and breathe!* It is one big muscular pump made up of involuntary muscle cell and is not heart-shaped at all. It will pump approximately 2000 gallons of blood throughout the body. Electrical impulses cause the heart to beat, and pressure created in the heart during a heartbeat is enough to squirt blood a distance of thirty feet. The average heart beats 72 times a minute, 100,000 times a day, 3,600,000 times a year, and 2.5 billion times during a 70-year life span. It will pump enough blood to fill 100 swimming pools. The average man's heart weighs 10-12 oz. compared to 8-10 oz. for a woman. Your system of blood vessels—the arteries, veins, and capillaries—is over 60,000 miles long and would stretch around the world more than twice.

Simply stated, this is the way the heart works: The heart has 4 chambers, 2 superior atria, and 2 inferior ventricles. Blood flows into the right atrium and through the tricuspid valve into the right ventricle. From here it is

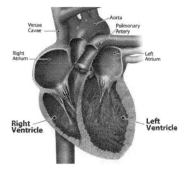

pumped to the lungs to dispose of CO2 and pick up O2. Next the oxygenated blood is pumped into the left atrium and then to the left ventricle, through the bicuspid valve. Finally, it is pumped out of the left ventricle to the body via the aorta. Arteries carry oxygenated blood away from the heart to the muscle cells. Veins carry deoxygenated blood back to the heart. Blood takes about 20 seconds to circulate through the entire human body.

"For with the heart one believes and thus has righteousness and with the mouth one confesses and thus has salvation." Romans 10:10

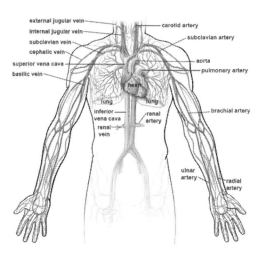

<u>Blood</u> – Did you know that in one square inch of your hand there are nine feet of blood vessels? There are 2.5 trillion (give or take) of red blood cells in your body at any moment. The average blood cell lives for 120 days. In order to maintain this number, about 2.5 million new ones need to be produced every second by your bone marrow. That's like a new population the size of the city of Toronto every second. A red blood cell can circumnavigate

your body in under 20 seconds. Our blood is on a 60,000-mile journey per day, and *our bodies give birth to 100 billion red cells every day!*

Christians believe that eternal life is granted by grace to all those who *personally* put their faith in the sacrificial death and shedding of blood of Jesus Christ on the cross for their sins. Likewise, our *earthly bodies* are also dependent upon the healthy flow of blood for life to continue.

> *"And almost all things are by the law purged with blood, and without shedding of blood is no remission."* Hebrews 9:22

Chapter Fifteen

Without Excuse

The reasons to believe in God as the *Intelligent Designer* of the universe and all that is in it are too numerous to list. But *Somebody Bigger* has attempted to cite *just a few God Wows* as a resource to help you persuade the *"nones"* to come to a saving faith in God and His only begotten Son, Jesus Christ. Here are a few final thoughts about why the *"nones"* are *WITHOUT EXCUSE...*

Think about it... God could have given us a black and white world, but he didn't. Instead, He painted our world and everything in it with an indescribable cacophony of color  from His infinite pallet. God's fingerprints are available for *ALL MEN TO SEE.*

He made every snowflake that has ever fallen on the landscapes of the earth an *original* design; and He molded every man, woman, and child into a *unique, purpose-filled* package. Just as it is impossible to count the snowflakes in a bank of

snow, it's also sheer folly trying to fathom the *infinite,* creative genius of the One who designed the universe and *everything* in it! God's majestic design is a daily, world-wide, wonderment of *"God-tweets"* telling us *how great our God is,* how much He loves us, and how much He desires to bring us into a loving relationship with His Son, Jesus Christ.

Take the lowly spider for example...one of God's most amazing and numerous creatures. One reason is that the un-born eggs of an entire egg sac of the spider outnumbers the population of India!

 Scientists also have discovered that a spider egg contains as much DNA as four humans combined. Added to this marvel of creative blueprint, God also included in the DNA of the spider's glands *the instructions for spinning a unique web every time.*

Another little known fact about spiders is that their shell— *if sufficiently scaled*—could adequately shield a nuclear blast. And there's an extremely rare spider in Eastern Africa, called the Snow Spider whose body is completely white, but it spins a completely black web. Reminds me of some *"nones"* who have developed a similarly *hardened shell* of resistance to the whispers of the Holy Spirit drawing them to a believing faith in

Christ. Instead, some prefer to remain caught in Satan's *black-web of deceit.*

Spiders also produce webs of fantastic materials, for example, the Copperhead Spider spins a web of *solid steel!* Some wonder if these insects could be used to repair airplanes or spacecraft while in flight. In 2001, space shuttle Atlantis (STS-98) carried a scientific package into orbit which included 300 spiders. Scientists are currently studying the spider as a potential treatment of several forms of cancer.

I leave you with one last sobering reminder to share with your non-believing friends and family members: *the death rate comes in at 100%!* According to the most recent stats taken from the Planetary Death Rate, 1.8 humans die every second, 106 every minute, 6,360 every hour, 152,640 every day, and 55,713,600 per year!

It is my prayer that *Somebody Bigger* will provide a handy informational resource to use as you share your personal story of faith with those outside Christ, who declares…

"I am the Lord your God and there is no other." Isaiah 45:5

"For since the creation of the world God's invisible qualities--his eternal power and divine nature--have been clearly seen, being understood from what has been made, so that people are <u>WITHOUT EXCUSE</u>." Romans 1:20

Chapter Research Sources

Chapter 1.

"Just By Chance...*they say, (article)* by Dr. Nita Weis

Chapter 2.

Genesis; Let Us Reason Ministries; All about Creation; Evidence for a Creator

Chapter 3.

Genesis; Various Science and Space websites

Chapter 4.

Genesis; *Reader's Digest*; World Water Council; New York Times; Florida Environmental Association; various "Water-related" websites

Chapter 5.

Genesis; NASA's *Imagine the Universe* website; Universe. com; National Academy of Science; Botanical Garden Conservation International; various Ecosystem, Environmental, and Botanical websites

Chapter 6.

Bible; Science of Bible Numerics; About.com/mathematics; Leonardo Pisano Fibonacci; *Fibonacci in Nature*, by Nikhat Parveen

Chapter 7.

Bible; DefendingGenesis.org; Messianic Prophecy Chart; Christsavesministries.org; and Thetrumpet.com

Chapter 8.

Bible; Christsavesministries.org; *Hope for Each Day*, by Billy Graham

Chapter 9.

Bible; *Grace for the Moment*, Vol. 2, by Max Lucado; various Space, Astronomy, Planetary, Solar System, and The Universe websites

Chapter 10.

Genesis; Catalogue of Life; World Register of Marine Species; various Marine Life, and Ornithology websites

Chapter 11.

Genesis; Dr. Adrian Rogers (sermon notes on Evolution: Fact or Fiction); Facts About Animals; Noah's Ark; AnswersinGenesis.org; *The Young Earth*, by John D. Morris, Ph.D.; *The New Answers Book 3*, by Tim Lovett & Bodie Hodge; various Christian and Animal websites

Chapter 12.

Genesis; Very Cool Facts about the Human Body; various Race, Language, Human Body, and Medical websites

Chapter 13.

Bible; *Signature in the Cell*, by Stephen C. Meyer; *Evolution: A Theory in Crisis*, by Michael Denton; *Fearfully & Wonderfully Made*, by Dr. Paul Brand & Philip Yancey; *Darwin's Black Box*, by Michael Behe; Intelligentdesign. org; Hypertexts for Biomedical Sciences; Biomimetics; Cell Biology; Physics; Cardiff University School of Bioscience, Physics, & Astronomy; and various other Intelligent-Design websites

Chapter 14.

Bible; Dr. Andrew Keller, Rockefeller University Professor; Advanced Hearing Group; Dr. David Jeremiah (Backbone); Hightechscience.org; How-it-works websites; various Human-Body Quick Facts; Medical websites on the Human Brain, the 5 Senses, Human Heart; Human Circulatory System

Chapter 15.

Bible; Federal Department of Spiders; Planetary Death Rate

All Chapters

Selected Information / quick facts from Ahmanson Lectures on Creation (Saddleback Church DVD Series); Bible translations used: KJV, NKJV, ASV, ESV, NIV, NET

Made in the USA
Charleston, SC
15 December 2014